BIPOC Alliances: Building Communities and Curricula

A Volume in:
Curriculum and Pedagogy

Series Editors:
The Curriculum and Pedagogy Group

Curriculum and Pedagogy

Series Editors:
The Curriculum and Pedagogy Group

Books in This Series:

*The Kaleidoscope of Lived Curricula: Learning Through a Confluence of
Crises 13th Annual Curriculum & Pedagogy Group 2021 Edited Collection* (2021)
Karin Ann Lewis, Kimberly Banda, Martha Briseno, and Eric J. Weber

*Making A Spectacle:
Examining Curriculum/Pedagogy as Recovery From Political Trauma* (2020)
Megan Ruby, Michelle Angelo-Rocha, Mark Hickey, and Vonzell Agosto

*Ideating Pedagogy in Troubled Times:
Approaches to Identity, Theory, Teaching and Research* (2019)
Shalin Lena Raye, Stephanie Masta, Sarah Taylor Cook, and Jake Burdick

Critical Intersections In Contemporary Curriculum & Pedagogy (2018)
Laura Jewett, Freyca Calderon-Berumen, and Miryam Espinosa-Dulanto

Collective Unravelings of the Hegemonic Web (2014)
Becky L. Noël Smith, Katherine Becker, Libbi R. Miller,
Natasha S. Reid, and Michele D. Sorensen

Liminal Spaces and Call for Praxis(ing) (2013)
Miryam Espinosa-Dulanto, David L. Humpal, Leilya Pitre, and Jolanta Smolen Santana

Excursions and Recursions: Through Power, Privilege, and Praxis (2012)
Brandon Sams, Jennifer Job, and James C. Jupp

*Surveying Borders, Boundaries, and Contested
Spaces in Curriculum and Pedagogy* (2011)
Cole Reilly, Victoria Russell, Laurel K. Chehayl, and Morna M. McDermott

BIPOC Alliances: Building Communities and Curricula

Indira Bailey
Christen Sperry García
Glynnis Reed
Leslie C. Sotomayor II

INFORMATION AGE PUBLISHING, INC.
Charlotte, NC • www.infoagepub.com

Library of Congress Cataloging-In-Publication Data

The CIP data for this book can be found on the Library of Congress website (loc.gov).

Paperback: 979-8-88730-057-3
Hardcover: 979-8-88730-058-0
E-Book: 979-8-88730-059-7

Copyright © 2023 Information Age Publishing Inc.

All rights reserved. No part of this publication may be reproduced, stored in a retrieval system, or transmitted, in any form or by any means, electronic, mechanical, photocopying, microfilming, recording or otherwise, without written permission from the publisher.

Printed in the United States of America

CONTENTS

Introduction vii
Indira Bailey, Leslie C. Sotomayor II,
Christen Sperry Garcia, and Glynnis Reed

PART I
TESTIMONIOS

1. **Testimonios And Microaggressions: BIPOC Student Experiences in Academia Through a Creative Collaborative Series of Letters** 3
   Leslie C. Sotomayor II, Kelvin K. Boakye, Maya Ilayne Kirkland, Bianca Isabela Rodriguez, and Chloe Grace Ferrer

2. **Claiming/Reclaiming Space: Chicana/x Latina/x Working Group (CLWG) Experience** 15
   Esther Medina De León

3. **Visual Testimonios: Artist/Writer Acts of Resistance and Recovery** 25
   Christen Sperry García, Leslie C. Sotomayor II, Alexis Marie Ramos, Elizabeth Gonzalez, Ricky Sullivan, Lourdes Garcia, Adilene Rosales, Rocio Guerrero, Mandy Wilson, and Nydia Salinas

4. Home, Family, and History: Highlighting an Underrepresented Geographic And Cultural Narrative...... 37
Gina Gwen Palacios

5. A Chicano-ish, Chicano, Chican@, or ChicanX Artist Statement 43
Paul Valadez

6. (Re)membering, (Re)constructing, and (Re)imagining Experience: Decolonizing Epistemological and Ontological Assumptions Formed in the Academy Through the Use of Autohistoria-Teoría in the Classroom 47
Kristin Alder

PART II
LIVED EXPERIENCES/IDENTITIES

7. Black Art Visuality: (Re)Directing the Black Gaze in Art Education 59
Indira Bailey

8. Paper Thin Boundaries 71
Glynnis Reed

9. When and Where I Enter: A Reflective Essay on the Photographic History of Three Generations of Black Women Educators 77
Meghan Green

10. ode to cymone and will (ode is a really white, really funny word) 85
Samuel Jaye Tanner

11. Defining "Belonging" in Classrooms: Collected Narratives From Two Educators in Art and Science at Higher Education Institutions 91
Kyungeun Lim and Soon Goo Lee

12. Centering Asian Women's Feminist Anger Using Zines in Art Education 103
Eunkyung Hwang

PART III
DE-CENTERING WHITE CURRICULAR CANONS

13. Witnessing Calls to Action: An Anti-Racist Education Through a Public Curriculum of the Arts.. 117
    Addyson Frattura and Yotam Ronen

14. Building Better Curriculum Through Black Hair............................ 129
    Linda Hoeptner Poling and Juliann Dorff

15. BIPOC Perspectives and Subaltern Voices: The Doubly Oppressed Subject of the Marginalized Feminist Artist.................. 141
    Maia Toteva

16. Disrupting and Transgressing the Canon: Including BIPOC Voices... 153
    Rochonda L. Nenonene, Novea A. McIntosh, and R. Darden Bradshaw

17. Reclaiming our Indigeneity: Deconstructing Settler Myths Through Micro-Activism 165
    Rosalva Resendiz, Lucas Enrique Espinoza, and Luis Enrique Espinoza

Contributors 175

INTRODUCTION

Indira Bailey
Claflin University

Leslie C. Sotomayor II
Texas Tech

Christen Sperry Garcia
The University of Texas Rio Grande Valley

Glynnis Reed
The Pennsylvania State University

COMING TOGETHER

We enter this co-edited book volume in the middle of a long conversation about missing voices and representation of the BIPOC community. Our roles as co-editors have been made possible because of all the other conversations that led to the fruition of this book. As four Women of Color who have grappled with our own positionalities within educational realms as learners, artists, instructors, and scholars, we have been having the same conversations for years in various ways. Feelings of not-belonging and othered in the academic canons because of the lack of representation within our programs, faculty, communities, and curriculum designs that have repeatedly failed us.

BIPOC Alliances: Building Communities and Curricula, pages ix–xv.
Copyright © 2023 by Information Age Publishing
www.infoagepub.com
All rights of reproduction in any form reserved.

We have drawn strength from each other throughout the years, forming panels, curating art exhibits, and community engagements, and designing syllabi that have not existed prior in these spaces. Because we have been acutely aware of our invisibility in educational institutions, scholarly literature, conferences, and art galleries, we continuously reached out to each other. We became bridges to support our points of connections to students and cultivated communities for our own survival. In our healing process, we witnessed again and again how we are not the only ones that feel this deep sense of not-belonging. As we continued to pool our resources together every semester, we collaborated with other underrepresented voices requiring support of resources to build a diversified curriculum and community in their respective places. A vocabulary emerged out of these gaps that we felt needed to produce new opportunities and possibilities through creative pedagogies that we each strive to implement in our own work. Our *testimonios* are our lived experiences that shaped and changed us in some way to bear witness to our interconnectivity (Anzaldúa & Keating, 2015; Collins, 2000; Keating, 2007). Through our lived experiences, we shape, give contact, and create meaning for our lives and how we relate to others.

WHAT IS MISSING

This book addresses the gaps of the historical exclusions that BIPOC individuals and collectives continuously feel. We witness this exclusion from academic canons continuously hyphenated with exceptionalities of exotified special topics celebrated like resistance work. We are often reminded in traditional canons, the over-served populations, that only a select few are capable of knowledge production and being voices of foundational proportions. However, we know that this is not true. The lack of representation *is* representation. When individuals are oppressed by systemic discrimination through their lives and intergenerational transmission, they may believe the stereotypes, myths, and derogatory social narratives about their own culture and identities communicated through the dominant media, education, institutions, and policies, among other means. Negative perceptions of oneself and one's cultural group normalizes a sense of subordinate status and can lead to internalized oppressions (Duran, 2013).

Through the re-envisioning of academic canons that have long governed course text selection to engage learners we engage in a process for decolonizing U.S. academic canons that are based on White supremacy. Our diverse voices can critically dismantle systemically internalized oppressions offering new possibilities for knowledge that have historically been silenced, buried, and ignored (Bhattacharya, 2013; Navas et al., 2017). As under-represented communities we have forged opportunities for collaboration specifically within Latina/x, Chicana/x and Black intersectional ties that arise from social issues such as race, socioeconomic status, gender, sex and sexualities. This book addresses how we are recognizing our dis-membered parts and re-membering parts of ourselves and communities. Therefore, we apply Maria Lugones's theory of decolonial feminism by discussing and approaching curriculum as spaces for multiple understandings or realities (Lugones, 2010). We position *testimonios* and lived experiences as an approach, a method, to conducting research and to bearing witness to learners' and our own experiences (Reyes & Rodríguez, 2012).

OUR AIM

We envision *BIPOC Alliances: Building Communities and Curricula* as a curated collection of reflective experiences, underrepresented voices, and alliances that confront, challenge, disrupt, and resist hegemonic academic canons as critical methodologies for empowerment (Reilly & Lippard, 2018). We situate our premise as holistic beings who all carry and share knowledge within ourselves. As we theorize about our lived experiences and create new narratives for ourselves and others, we enact Gloria Anzaldúa's autohistoria-teoría as a lens for decolonizing and theorizing one's own experiences or *testimonios* through creative acts, curriculum, writing, and sharing our stories (Anzaldúa & Keating, 2015).

We use pedagogical, curricular experiences, and *testimonios* as an approach, a methodology, to conduct research and to bear witness to learners' and one's own experiences (Reyes & Rodríguez, 2012). The authors selected provide *testimonios* or lived experiences decolonize academic canons and expand curricula and creative spaces to include BIPOC perspectives.

Our Lived Experiences/Testimonios

Indira

My history has been created and taught to me from a White perspective. Growing up and seeing negative images of Black people created by whites were disturbing. Where were my culture, my history, and my identity represented? I grew up in a black community that emphasized the rich legacy of African Americans. I listened to my elders describe their lived experiences living with Jim Crow laws, sitting in the back of a bus, civil rights protests, working as domestic workers in white households, and limited education. These stories told from generation to generation were excluded or ignored in my education, which intrigued my desire to learn more about my own culture. As a descendant of enslaved Africans, I realize that if I do not tell our stories and traditions through the arts, another person will.

I draw my scholarship from a Black feminist perspective (Collins, 2000) after witnessing and experiencing sexism and racism due to my race and gender. African American women experience a spectrum of intersectional oppressions. Where do I go? Who will listen to my voice when I don't fit the checklist of underrepresented categories of being a black man or a white woman? My intersectional experiences of being silenced, ignored, and excluded have left me questioning my identity and self-worth. I aim to empower African American women's ideas, voice, and existence in the arts and academia.

Leslie

As an American-born Latina student, I observed very little, if any, representation or acknowledgement of my hyphenated Caribbean ethnic background throughout my education from kindergarten through college. I began to understand that my educational disadvantages, as an underserved ESL student attending over-represented educational institutions throughout my life, had helped me to develop coping skills. One of the ways that I became self-empowered was to look to my ancestral roots from Puerto Rico and Cuba as places for self-discovery through testimonio, art and writing. Implementing a decolonizing feminist approach, autohistoria-teoría and conocimiento, I was able to theorize my own process for healing and witness students' process as well (Sotomayor, 2022).

Throughout my life I have struggled and grappled with the label of whiteness, being identified as either white or woman of color depending on where I am geographically positioned in the Caribbean or the U.S. and who is standing next to me. I realize that my experiences are not isolated nor uncommon. I witness it often in the classroom spaces I inhabit as educator, curator, artist and writer. The borders that I consistently cross through my intersectional identity, I am unpacking as I am constantly negotiating contradictions of fragmentation and wholeness while resisting modes of patriarchy (Keating, 2015).

Christen

I am a Chicana from the San Diego/Tijuana US/Mexico borderlands. The tensions and contradictions that I negotiate are those between the US/Mexico borderlands and the borderlands of education. My educational experiences are a borderlands patchwork. Attending and teaching at both PWI and HSI institutions, I was not introduced to borderlands theories, Critical Race Theory, or the work of Gloria Anzaldúa until I entered a PhD program at a PWI. Like many artists and scholars, I have had to teach myself about many artists of color and their methodologies, including Latina/x artists (Dávila, 2020).

I have had to reflect on, resist, and counter what I was *taught* so I could learn from a new perspective. For example, as a student at an HSI, I was *taught* that I was inferior to other students at "better schools," that I would not be as successful as those at other PWI art schools that surrounded the art metropolis of Los Angeles. I was *taught* that because we were largely a first-generation college bound school that we would not amount to much. I was *taught* to look at myself through a deficit model. I was *taught* to never make art about my identity as a Latina/Chicana/Mexican American/Hispanic woman because I would not be taken seriously and I would be pigeon-holed as a Chicana artist, not an artist (subtext is White). Now is my time to *unteach* what I have been *taught*.

Glynnis

As an African American queer woman artist with an invisible disability, I am invested in critical inquiry as a tool of personal liberation and intellectual exploration (Lorde, 1984). I am a Ph.D. candidate in Art Education and Women's, Gender, and Sexuality Studies at a PWI. I was born and raised in Los Angeles and have been based in New Jersey for twelve years. My intersectional identities grant me an awareness that urges me to center the experiences of communities marginalized by differences in race, gender, sexuality, and disability through my roles as scholar, researcher, educator, and artist. My multilayered identities offer great richness to my life, adding much depth and dimension to my everyday reality (Lorde, 1984). Education has been key for me in unlocking my full potential and the abundance of my personal gifts throughout my life; the pursuit of my doctoral degree has been liberating for me as well.

Because of the marginalization I experience personally, I am highly motivated to develop tools through writing and critical analysis that will help me to dismantle the effects of oppression in my own life and be able to guide others on their personal and academic journeys. Through academic study, I can create new structures for myself to maneuver in and through. I hold the awareness of the difficulties that my African American ancestors have gone through. I believe I am doing the work for them and other women who came before me who did not have opportunities to articulate or actualize their freedom to be, to learn, to live, to love to their full capacity.

LAYOUT OF BOOK

We organized *BIPOC Alliances* into three sections: testimonios, lived experiences/identities, and de-centering white curricular canons. Each section includes creative chapters that engage the theorizing of lived experiences in some capacity through academic scholarship, research, and creative work.

Part 1: Testimonios

In Part one, authors share their testimonios and bear witness to one another's experiences (Reyes & Rodríguez, 2012). Sharing their stories and engaging in autohistoria-teoría, theorizing through lived experiences (Anzaldúa & Keating, 2015), students, teachers, artists, scholars, and those that fit in-between these career designations, share their classroom, artist, family, and personal life experiences. Living on/in/within a geographical, metaphorical, or psychic borderlands (Anzaldúa, 2012; Anzaldúa & Keating, 2015), the authors use text, poetry, and visual art to perform creative acts of *nepantlando*. The process of nepantlando combines nepantla, an ideological space of living in-between worlds with "ando" and action verb in Spanish that means "-ing" (Sotomayor & García, 2022). Moving from ideology to action, nepantlando is a creative act of working through living in-between worlds. Through nepantlando, these writers/artists engage in visual testimonio works.

Part 2: Lived Experiences/Identities

Part two draws attention to the lived experiences and identities that address race in academia, visual culture, and curricula. This section highlights lived experiences as an act of resistance in developing individual points of view to express oppression and challenge the white narrative believed and taught (Collins, 2000). The author's lived experiences deconstruct formal education as the only source of knowledge and invoke scholarship to investigate other forms of pedagogical practices and methodologies. The authors execute their right to describe their reality, establish their identity, and define their history in relation to their lived experiences through artwork, photographs, and poetry (hooks, 1992). Being vulnerable is demonstrated by the sharing of personal stories through (re)shifting Black art visuality, Black feminist identities, the lens of daughtering, disrupting white supremacy, and anti-Asian racism (Brantmeier & McKenna, 2020). The lived experiences shared are a collective act of empowerment.

Part 3: De-centering White Curricular Canons

The authors in Part Three seek to actively disrupt White hegemonic narratives in education through the development of curricula and pedagogy as resistance and activism. Understanding the importance of transparency about the situatedness associated with one's personal identity, several of the authors frame their writing in relation to their positionalities. In their work to de-center White canons and to critique white supremacy, several authors included in this section express how one's subjective position based on race and ethnicity hold significant weight in the articulation of our perspectives on educational practices. Other forms of oppression are critical to engage in contemporary culture as well, such as heteronormativity, heterosexism, patriarchy, and classism, particularly due to the way they impact multiple marginalized individuals. These writings reflect activism focused on identity in the struggle to create more opportunities for all through powerful engagements with learning.

REFERENCES

Anzaldúa, G. (2012). *Borderlands/La frontera: The new mestiza* (4th ed.). Aunt Lute Books.
Anzaldúa, G., & Keating, A. (2015). *Luz en lo oscuro: Rewriting identity, spirituality, reality.* Duke University Press.
Bhattacharya, K. (2013). Performing gender as "Third-World-Other" in higher education: De/colonizing transnational feminist possibilities. *Creative Approaches to Research,* 6(3), 30–43.
Brantmeier, E. J., & McKenna, M. (2020). Pedagogy of vulnerability: Roots, realities and the future. In E. J. Brantmeir & M. McKenna (Eds.), *Pedagogy of vulnerability* (pp. 1–24). Information Age Publishing.
Collins, P. (2000). *Black feminist thought: Knowledge, consciousness, and the politics of empowerment.* Routledge.
Dávila, A. (2020). *Latinx art: Artists, markets, and politics.* Duke University Press.

Duran, E. J. R. (Ed.). (2013). *Internalized oppression: The psychology of marginalized groups*. Springer.
hooks, b. (1992). *Black looks: Race and representation*. South End Press.
Keating, A. (2007). *Teaching transformation. Transcultural classroom dialogues*. Springer.
Lorde, A. (1984). *Sister outsider. The Crossing Press feminist series.* Penguin Books.
Lugones, M. (2010). Toward a decolonial feminism. *Hypatia, 25*(4), 742–759.
Navas, E., Gallagher, O., & Burrough, X. (2017). *Keywords in remix studies* (1st ed.). Taylor & Francis.
Reilly, M., & Lippard, L. R. (2018). *Curatorial activism: Towards an ethics of curating*. Thames & Hudson.
Reyes, K. B., & Rodríguez, J. E. (2012). Testimonio: Origins, terms, and resources. *Equity & Excellence in Education, 45*(3), 525–538. doi: 10.1080/10665684.2012.698571
Sotomayor, L. (2022). *Teaching in/between: Curating educational spaces with autohistoria—Teoría and conocimiento*. Vernon Press.
Sotomayor, L., & García, C. S. (Forthcoming, 2022). Nepantlando: Visual teaching through curadora methodology. In A. S. Alexander & M. Sharma (Eds.), *Routledge companion to decolonizing art, craft, and visual culture education*. Routledge.

PART I

TESTIMONIOS

CHAPTER 1

TESTIMONIOS AND MICROAGGRESSIONS

BIPOC Student Experiences in Academia Through a Creative Collaborative Series of Letters

Leslie C. Sotomayor II
Texas Tech University

Kelvin K. Boakye, Maya Ilayne Kirkland,
Bianca Isabela Rodriguez, and Chloe Grace Ferrer
Texas Tech University

The position of underrepresented students in academia in relation to their host campuses—as influenced by social capital, socio-economic status, marginalization, and stereotyping impacts learner's intersectional realities and their sense of belonging or lack thereof (Hurtado & Carter, 1997; Strahorn, 2012). In curating inclusionary learning experiences that resist and challenge Anglo culture and academic canons, we may empower underrepresented students to reconnect with their cultures and cultivate their own roots and experiences. Curating educational environments offers opportunities to engage in exposure of wounds and healing through creative acts (Anzaldúa, 2015). I highlight here, with BIPOC undergraduate practicum learners and co-authors, the importance for the process of active listening, and supporting learners who continually feel a sense of in-betweenness and not-belonging by initiating a process for healing through collective consciousness and vulnerability (Sotomayor, 2022). The act of writing about marginalized experiences as an embodied experience is an act of resistance and unlearning, decolonizing.

THEORIZING TO (UN)LEARN

Students decided to write collaboratively largely informed by testimonio work as self-identifying BIPOC individuals. Theorizing through the work of bell hooks (2000),[1] reading the creative book chapters of Clelia Rodriguez (2018),[2] and having reflected on testimonio work through Gloria Anzaldúa (2015)[3] the students were able to tease out approaches which in turn were embodied through creative writing. Most of the discussions about the formatting and content for the chapter were done as a group where I mostly listened and offered resources to view or read. Students considered writing a more academic chapter that centered on theorizing about their experiences. However, after engaging Rodriguez's book[4] they felt inspired to use a letter format for their chapter. Students enacted a process of actively listening and went from shy observations and recounting experiences to deep-diving conversations with each other, me, and even branched out to share and discuss with family members about their lived experiences.

In the letters that follow, student's theorized about their experiences by applying feminist theories into their writing and reflections about their experiences.

PART I. KELVIN

Dear (Redacted),

Do you remember the first time you stepped off that plane, and into this country?

---

[1] bell hook's (2000) theorizes and engages with her writing by intentionally writing in a way that is accessible to most versus catering to higher education or academic modes of language. She does this by not conflating her writing with academic jargon but rather chooses to use a language vocabulary that is relatable and accessible to general populations. In this vein, the student's letters to follow in this chapter are not weighed down by academic vernacular but rather are written in 'plain' everyday language to theorize about their lived experiences.

[2] Clelia Rodriguez (2018) disrupts the academic writing canon through creative and decolonizing/unlearned practices. In Rodriguez's book, she chooses to write several chapters as creative letters that although adhere to some modes of traditional letter writing with a greeting, body and sign-off, it is disrupted by the creative liberty with use of text and symbols, fonts and letter sizes, various lengths, and a repetitive pattern of writing many letters to constitute a chapter. In choosing the creative writing style of letters, each student was able to share their story in a consistent medium although each is quite different in the creative execution of their letter. Students were able to write to a person/entity of their choosing, sharing whatever they felt was most important.

[3] Gloria Anzaldúa, (2015) created her own theory of autohistoria-teoría as a decolonizing feminist writing practice of testimonio as an opportunity to curate self-knowledge, belonging, community building through self-empowerment.

[4] Rodriguez, C. (2018). Decolonizing Academia.

Do you remember how sweat-soaked your armpits and how insecurity gripped your heart? The feeling of being in an unknown land, a singular drop in the middle of a vast ocean. Sitting in an airport with people passing by, feeling their disapproving eyes boring into you and seeping into your very soul. How you clung to the hands of your siblings, who had come to be your only comfort on this long exhausting journey. And it WAS long, and it WAS exhausting. But here you were, in the land of freedom and opportunity.

Do you remember the feeling of seeing your parents after three, almost four years of separation? How you longed to weep in your mother's arms. Cry all the tears you had been holding back all those years you were without her. How you wished to hold on to your father and breathe in his scent for you had started to forget what your own father smelled like. How you wished to hold your newest sibling, whom you had never met a day before in your life. Your little brother whom you shamefully resented, for he had your parents when you most needed them, and this knowledge ate at you like acid.

Do you remember how in the back seat of the car, surrounded by your family, that initial feeling of alienation faded to a barely noticeable hum in the back of your brain?

If you only knew.

Being new anywhere is daunting. However, being the new kid who just immigrated from an unknown African country, in a class with no other black people in the middle of the school year, well that is a different kind of isolation.

I remember my first day of school very clearly. The sense of impending doom as I walked down the hall with my principal and my mother towards my very first class in a new country. Quietly standing in front of a sea of eyes as my teacher introduced me to the class. The feeling of dread as I scanned the room for anyone who looked like me, the sinking feeling as I realized I was essentially alone. I remember the curious gaze with which my new classmates looked at me, I hated it.

I was never aware of my skin color, of course, this might be because I was still a child, nonetheless, I did not become aware of my skin until immigrating to this country. I went from being surrounded by people who looked like me to being suddenly not. Now El Paso is far from being a white suburbia, and the city has a healthy African population, but this does not change the fact that I felt, and sometimes still feel, lonely. Always one of two or three black kids in a classroom in schools with less than 100 black students and not a single black teacher from 4th–12th grade, I missed the feeling of community that Ghana provided.

Where Are You From?
I'm from Ghana

Oh My Gosh That's Really Cool.
Yeah, I guess

Have You Ever Seen a Lion, Giraffe, Cheetah...?
Not really, I lived in a city

Where Did You Learn to Speak English So well?
IDK I guess I've always spoken English

How Do You Say Your Last Name?
Boakye, pronounced Bo-a-che

I'm Sorry How Do You Say It Again? That's Really Complicated How About I Just Say It This Way Instead?
Oh....Ok

I've lost track of how many times I've heard a variation of these questions. The first time somebody asked me if I had ever seen a lion up close, I thought they were joking, and maybe they were, so I laughed and replied, no that's crazy. They then went on to keep badgering me with questions and as the interrogation continued, I got more and more uncomfortable. I thought I was being dramatic after all; these are just harmless questions. But no matter how hard I tried to convince myself these comments weren't serious, the more the feeling of discomfort grew.

Eventually, I began to assimilate into the culture that I was thrust into, and the comments stopped being thrown at me and an entirely different beast took their place. I'd always been aware of my black skin, but I'd never thought that the skin I'd had all my life could have negative connotations. Being in this country has made me hyperaware of my skin and the dangers that come with it.

And so, I grew, and I made my way through a land of unknowns with my skin which had become synonymous with danger. A walking, flashing, neon warning sign. And I tried to be "different," tried to change, be quieter, less black, less Ghanian. I gradually lost my accent and stopped telling people that I was an immigrant and started saying I was from El Paso, Dallas, Houston, anything really to get them to stop talking to me. And it worked! The comments changed...but the discomfort did not.

You're one of the good ones....
Thanks, I guess

You're not like other black people
I don't know what that means.

You're a credit to your race
Lol....ok

From K

PART II. BIANCA

Dear Bianca,

To be younger in a classroom surrounded by people that look like you.

Not having to be worried about feeling disconnected from others or feeling like an outcast.

My neighborhood in the Southeast side of Houston has always made me feel socially comfortable, because my neighborhood is a Hispanic neighborhood. I felt comfortable, not viewing myself as a minority nor setting myself in this category society tends to put us in. As a little girl, I never saw myself being put in situations of fearing harassment by fellow peers in the classroom or school campus settings.

It wasn't until the eighth grade when I started to see a shift in who was sitting next to me in the classroom. I had just moved from Houston ISD to Pasadena ISD for a better curriculum and education. The curriculum was quite different, beforehand I was always in the "gifted and talented" classrooms or pre-AP classes. I was used to learning fast-paced classrooms and being able to notice material quickly. I still remember the first day of eighth grade for me, feeling shy and scared I would not fit in or be smart enough. I remember sitting in front of my algebra class so eager to learn. I was so confident I would be up to date on the material. The teacher had already begun teaching Unit one and I was so confused and felt like I was already so behind. I was so quick to see how the other kids around me were so ahead, Houston ISD curriculum had not prepared me.

In the social aspect I was so used to going to school in BIPOC communities that the transfer of schools was a culture shock. I isolated myself the first couple months after the transfer. The popular group of girls at this intermediate school were all white. I endured the ugly looks from them and the small whispers when I walked by them every day. They had never spoken to me. I started to question why I was so hated by them. Was it because I dressed differently? Was it because of the color of my skin? Was it because I did not look like them?

My sense of belonging did get much better in high school. I was able to meet more Hispanic peers due to the integration of middle schools for ninth grade. I felt more like myself again. I didn't feel as judged for the way I looked or how I presented myself to others. My sense of belonging got better, but I was still uncomfortable at times. My high school was predominantly a Hispanic community, but I still felt the frowning upon us. The word "**beaner**" was thrown around like nothing. You would hear the occasional "**wet back**" being thrown around as well. I felt ashamed when hearing these derogatory terms being used so regularly and carelessly.

Since High school it just got worse. I thought college would be much different in a good way. You always see college in the movies pictured as so much fun, a time for you to get to learn more about yourself and meet lifelong friends. Although it has been all of the above, I wasn't mentally prepared for the blatant racism I would have to endure in Lubbock, Texas. Such as the time during my first semester I was at a football game with my brother and our friends. I was told by a fellow white female university student

'Go back to Mexico'

'If you don't like it here, you should cross the wall.'

'Go back to where you came from.'

Nine hours away from what I was so used to.

Being harassed by a fellow peer of my institution. A place where I should feel comfortable trying to pursue a degree for not only myself, but my family. Growing up I saw both of my parents work so hard to provide for my brother and me. I have always been so grateful for not only what they have done, but what my grandparents have done as well. My Güeli, Guelo, Tamom, and Guelo Chevy (my grandparents) immigrated to the United States leaving their families in the pursuit of a better life for their children and themselves. I will never be ashamed to state that I come from an immigrated family. However, I will say, I do find it hard to be in a small town surrounded by people who aren't ashamed to belittle others about where they come from.

Freshwoman attending a university campus that is consider a "Hispanic serving institution." It astonished me when moving to Lubbock how the campus does not even seem like it is an HSI, it feels like a predominantly white institution (PWI). As I walk into my classrooms, I find myself scoping the classroom for fellow people of color students. I'd be lucky if I could say I could find more than five peers of color in one classroom.

There are things that I have learned this past semester living in Lubbock that bother me. Such as struggling to find authentic Hispanic food in Lubbock, going to the grocery store and not finding the Hispanic foods I like to eat, the lack of POC professors at my institution, receiving harsh looks when speaking Spanish in public, being told by white males I am too aggressive because of the Latina in me and especially not being able to connect with some of my closest friends on certain values. I hate that I can't express how I feel on certain social topics with friends because they are deemed as political and god forbid, we speak on politics with one another.

These are struggles I face daily.

Being a Latina in society isn't always easy, but through the rough times I can always hear my mom in the back of my head telling me **'¡You are a chingona, si se puede!..'**

PART III. CHLOE

To Chloe's Younger Self,

Don't be ashamed of your differences.

Embrace them.

Don't look for ways to blend in and assimilate.

Embrace yourself.

In the fourth grade, I was assigned a school project of researching and creating a poster about the country our families came from.

I remember choosing Germany.

It was between Germany and France.

European countries like everyone else in my predominately white fourth grade class, were researching.

Why didn't I want to embrace my culture and research the Philippines?

Since the fourth grade, I haven't been ashamed of being Filipino, I love being Filipino, Filipino cuisine, and Filipino hospitality.

I just have never been taught the "right" way to embrace this part of myself.

I now know there is no 'right' way to do this.

No universal answer because no one's experience is the same.

Growing up, I wasn't taught to ignore my Filipino culture.

But when my dad immigrated to the United States from the Philippines when he was 10 years old, his parents decided to stop speaking in their native tongues; Tagalog and Visayan.

My Lolo and Lola, wanting to save my dad and his sister from being bullied because of their Asian-ness in Southeast Louisiana, sacrificed a part of themselves because the language couldn't be passed on to their children and grandchildren.

So, I grew up in mostly every other aspect of myself: white.

Sometime around fourth grade, I found myself in Social Studies class 'popcorn' reading about the Civil War.

I've always been a shy kid.

When discussing this topic as a class, I remember when a classmate quoted that "yeah, we don't hate Chloe."

We don't hate Chloe. We don't hate Chloe. We don't hate...

I remember shamefully covering myself and embarrassment heating up my cheeks.

I didn't like being the center of attention, I was first trying to process being singled out in front of the class.

Looking back, it was a pivotal moment for me.

My classmate had assumed I was African American because of my brown skin.

This is the first instance I can remember being conscious of my different color of skin compared to my classmates.

The first time being put into a situation of explaining to someone else how my father is Filipino, and my mother is white.

Of putting my cultural identity into words.

Of feeling self-conscious and dismissive towards myself.

Yet being a source of fascination and curiosity to others.

I have always struggled between not being 'enough' Filipino or 'enough' White.

Or even knowing the right way to correct people when they assume I am Hispanic, Malaysian, Polynesian or just "exotic."

Of being biracial but not understanding my brownness.

Of feeling inauthentic in my own body.

Of the constant imposters syndrome.

Feeling like I don't act Filipino enough, but I don't look white enough either.

And the questions.

*"WHAT **ARE** YOU?"*
*"**WHERE** ARE YOU FROM?"*
*"WHERE ARE YOU **REALLY** FROM?"*
*"OH, **ARE YOU SURE** YOUR MOM IS WHITE?"*

The internal awkwardness I experience while I attempt to answer these questions.

But

I

have

never

been more aware of my cultural identity since coming to university in Lubbock, Texas.

My institution is defined as a Hispanic Serving Institution.

But it doesn't always feel like one.

I can count on one hand the number of professors I've had who were a person of color.

My Mexican friends don't believe me when I tell them a quarter of the student body is Hispanic.

I've never felt more invisible walking into a frat party with my friends who are Mexican and Filipino.

I have this hyper-awareness of who I surround myself with now, in school and in life.

When entering a classroom, at the beginning of a semester, I find myself scoping out the people inside.

Is it predominantly white kids?

Or is it diverse?

It isn't until I've forced myself to still and examine my personal identities that I am finding the words to describe this battle between these two parts of me.

Of accepting there is no 'right' way to be myself.

Of wanting to learn more about my Filipino culture.

Of recognizing my buried bitterness, I have towards my dad for not fighting harder to 'be more Filipino.'

Because maybe then I would have a stronger certainty towards this part of myself. And, to my younger self, I would say embrace yourself in any way that feels right.

Don't do what everyone else in fourth grade is doing for that project.

Don't feel forced to be a certain way or fit an impossible standard of being exactly half one 'thing' and half 'another.'

There is no perfect way to do this.

The longer you try looking for this perfect way is time wasted.

But don't shy away from your differences, and don't be afraid to call people out who make wrong assumptions about you based on how you look.

I am still learning.

Rooting for you always,

Chlo

PART IV. MAYA

Dear Unassuming Parents,

To give me a better education and save me from the life I was destined to have, my parents made the questionable decision to send me and my brother to a private Christian school in the city. Looking back, I understand why. My sister was 18, pregnant, and a drug addict and when they looked at me, they saw her. I was overjoyed to be attending a new school, but I never thought the five years I spent there would cause me to have an internalized hatred for myself, lasting to this day.

August 5th, 2009, was the first time my intellect was questioned. I was a smart kid and had finished the admissions exam in under an hour. This granted me a scholarship and automatic admission for my brother. However, before I could even introduce myself to the class, I was paired with a white student, and told that when I had questions, to ask her. It was the first day of third grade, how could I have been behind? A couple of months into school and I was being praised for how well I was doing. However, my 6-year-old brother had already been sent to the principal's office 3 times. Reasons cited as "His ADHD is distracting. He needs to be medicated or taken out of my class." This was the first of many infractions.

I quickly based my whole life on being the quiet and reliable one. This is how I would stay out of trouble, this is how I would be deemed good, this is how I would not be like him. I felt sorry for my brother because he did not understand the game yet. To be liked, to be loved, you must be what they want you to be. Therefore, I needed to be perfect. I tried to teach my brother how to do it. How to shut up, listen and keep your head down. That is how they wanted us to be, but he was different.

I was the better Kirkland. 4 years at this school and I had successfully been nothing like him. I felt loved by teachers, while he felt attacked. Only in 5th grade but he was already a regular in the In-School Suspension room. Jumping fences to get tennis balls, taking too long in the bathroom, not sharing the basketball at recess, his rap sheet was long and ever-growing. It was hard being his sister. Being questioned as to why we were so different. Now that he was older and there was no chance, he would be anything like me, I was now his keeper.

'Watch out for your *brother* at school!
Keep your *brother* out of trouble.
Help your *brother* with his homework!
Talk to that teacher about your *brother*.
Don't forget to wake your *brother* up for school.'
My feverish need to be perfect had caught up with me. I set the bar too high.

I hated my brother. He was too loud. He was too annoying. He cannot sit still. He was so dumb. He cursed too much. He was so mean. He is so Black.

This is What a PWI Did to Me

Not a single Black teacher or administrator. One of four Black students in my grade. One of less than 100 in the entire K–12 school. I had changed myself so much to fit in, I hated my brother for refusing to do so. I did not see myself as a Black person, only a person who sadly was black.

My brother was not any of those things, he was just a happy little boy. He was **not** the only one talking
he was **not** the only one being a disruption.
But he was the only Black kid, and he was the only one threatened with expulsion at 6 for a lack of an ADHD medication prescription.
He was **not** the only kid jumping fences and hogging basketballs.
He was doing it with his friends.
But he was the only Black kid, and he was the only one in ISS.
He was **not** the only kid checking out books in the library after school and
he was **not** the only one returning them to the drop-box area.
But he was the only Black kid, and he was the only one cornered by teachers and dragged to the principal's office.
He was the only one accused of stealing school property.
He was the only one expelled on the spot.
And he was the only one who did not receive an apology when they found said book in the drop-box area that same day.

We were different. I was who they wanted me to be, he was who he wanted to be. I wish I could go back and scream in my ear 'Take care of him, this world is not safe for him. He will not get by as easily as you will.' I wish I could take every experience in this essay and remove it from his memory so he will never know the pain of being vilified for being himself. But I cannot, so I will fight for change, so this does not happen to next little Black boy, and his quiet older Black sister.

Sincerely,

The one who found her way

THE CULMINATION OF THIS CHAPTER

In this chapter, we situate autohistoria-teoría as a form of curating to embody and engage with a healing process because of underrepresented life stories not being part of dominant cultural discourses or academic canons causing underrepresented populations to often feel an intense sense of not-belonging (Sotomayor, 2022). As student's reflected, questioned, interrogated, and theorized about some of their lived experiences, they were able to engage and enact a self-healing process and a collective response to each other and themselves.[5]

---

[5] These stages of reflection were important in order to get to a place where they could share their stories with each other, family members, writing and culminating into a presentation about their work at the Texas Tech University Women's and Gender Studies spring conference (2022).

REFERENCES

Anzaldúa, G. (2015). *Light in the dark: Luz en lo oscuro: Rewriting Identity, spiritualty, reality*. (A. Keating, Ed.). Duke University Press.

Anzaldúa, G., & Keating, A. (2009). *The Gloria Anzaldúa reader*. Duke University Press.

Bhattacharya, K., & Keating, A. (2018). Expanding beyond public and private realities: Evoking Anzaldúan autohistoria-teoría in two voices. *Qualitative Inquiry, 24*(5), 345–354.

hooks, b. (2000). *Feminism is for everybody: Passionate politics*. Pluto Press.

Hurtado, S., & Carter, D. F. (1997). Effects of college transition and perceptions of the campus racial climate on Latino college students' sense of belonging. *Sociology of Education, 70*(4), 324–345.

Koshy, K. (2006). Nepantlera-activism in the transnational moment: In dialogue with Gloria Anzaldúa's theorizing of nepantla. *Human Architecture: Journal of the Sociology of Self-Knowledge, 4*(3), 147–161.

Navas, E., Gallagher, O., & Burrough, X. (2017). *Keywords in remix studies* (1st ed.). Taylor and Francis.

Rodríguez, C. O. (2018). *Decolonizing academia: Poverty, oppression and pain*. Fernwood Publishing.

Sotomayor, L. (2022). *Teaching in/between: Curating educational spaces with autohistoria—Teoría and conocimiento*. Vernon Press.

Strayhorn, T. L. (2012). *College students' sense of belonging: A key to educational success for all students*. Routledge.

CHAPTER 2

CLAIMING/RECLAIMING SPACE

Chicana/x Latina/x Working Group (CLWG) Experience

Esther Medina De León
Texas Tech University

Chicanas have long invested in creating spaces to provide safe spaces, discuss gender issues and ways to "disrupt patriarchal and organizational constructs, and to be heard and validated" (Espinoza, Cotera, Blackwell, 16). The creation of these spaces allowed for dialogue regarding Chicana Feminism. In Fall of 2019, the Chicana/x Latina/x Working Group. CLWG, was formed. As tenured faculty, I leveraged the group to provide participants ways to claim/reclaim spaces for themselves and others. This chapter discusses how CLWG was formed and progressed and the importance of creating connections, hermanidad (Espinoza, Cotera, Blackwell 16), comadrazgo—companionship, maternal/familial, a mentorship. The group was/is a space and however it is needed, a *neplantera, mestizaje,* a transformative space, not necessarily in one realm or another where these types of interactions occur.

I am not the first Chicana nor Latina librarian. Hopefully, I won't be the last. The first nationally recognized Chicana librarian is Elizabeth Martinez of California. Reading her memoir, *A Jaguar in the Library*, I felt a kind of kinship to her (Martinez, 2020). You would never think librarian-world would have anything to do with friendship, betrayals, challenges—it sounds somewhat like a *tela-novela*. But, as a Latina/Chicana, when we rise and ask for what is ours, to represent our culture, our people, we are often met with adversity, as expressed in her book. Martinez's story is different in that she was a real activist, like *dura*. If it were me back then, I would not know what to do. Back then, when the *movimientos* happened, our people were met with much more than just dissent. Similarly, as it was for her, through my own journey in academia as a tenured faculty/librarian, I had to learn about power struggles and fear in the workplace. I am her; she is me—except she was fighting for equity and inclusion in a public library whereas I am in an academic library/institution realm. Her words, "I became the spokesperson for diversity," resonated with me. I have become such a person within the library for diverse communities (Martinez, 2020). As Martinez claimed, what we learn in graduate school, and in general, about libraries—that they are free and for everybody—has not been and is not always true. An academic library, for example, especially a public institution, gets much of their funding from student-use fees. Consequently, libraries like these are more conscientious in their spending, making allowances for resources that are based on statistics and not necessarily what students and faculty need or want for their research or teaching. Elizabeth Martinez asks, (2020)," How could I possibly represent or be responsible for our entire culture, one so diverse within itself?" She writes that what she learned from the Chicano Movimiento is that "we needed an activist to throw the rock through the window to lead the path of change" and found out she was the rock; and, likewise, I am that rock (Martinez, 2020).

While working in academia, I have always thought, if not me, then who? Who else would serve in various capacities that serve the Chicana/o/x Latina/o/x communities? Although I was not the only faculty/staff representing the Latinx culture, the experiences I reflect on are my own and are through my own lens. Because of the need for more outspoken representation, as in programming, literature, materials, and resources that were crucial to student faculty and staff, it, the rock, became me. I created programs, exhibits, ofrendas, requested databases and book purchases in the library, for the Latinx and BIPOC communities. After a Hispanic Heritage Month program, a student approached me, and my career took an interesting, challenging, but necessary, turn. As referenced before, Latina/o/x, Chicana/o/x, and sometimes Hispanic, will be used interchangeably throughout this dialogue between you and I, to bring across my thoughts that I am trying to relay.

THE EMERGENCE OF THE CLWG—
CHICANA/X LATINA/X WORKING GROUP

The opportunity to create and provide a space, the CLWG, and to pay it forward (Ramirez 304) arose, as I was wrapping up the Hispanic Heritage month event in the Fall of 2018. I was approached by Corina Alvarado, a doctoral candidate, now co-PI, and was asked if I would help her with a grant proposal to create the working group. The Texas Tech University's (TTU) Humanities Center accepted and funded the proposal and have been incredibly supportive in our plight. We proposed that having this group was integral to the university because TTU, at the time, met requirements to achieve designation as a Hispanic Serving Institute (HSI) in 2019. TTU's *Fact Book*[1] website and Division of Diversity, Equity, and Inclusion's website noted the university's HSI designation process began in 2017 with 27.8% identifying Hispanics. Since the time of designation, the university has grown in number in total student population (over 40,000) and Hispanic students (29% or over 10,000). Of this number, it is important to note the number of Hispanic women in 2020 were 5,643, which is over half of the total number of Hispanics. Total Hispanic faculty on campus was 167, and Hispanic women faculty was 87, at time of designation. Total Hispanic faculty in 2020 was 168 and total Hispanic women was eighty-six showing total Hispanic faculty growth as minimal. Library representation is even sadder with 2020 total faculty sitting at 37, total Hispanic faculty 3, and only 2 who were tenured. It is also important to note that these numbers do not include those who identify as other, non-binary, non-gendered, nor does it reflect specific identities within "Hispanic" label, meaning those who are Hispanic, but do not identify as Hispanic. Also note that because of the low rise in faculty of color, especially that of Hispanic, Latina/o/x or Chicana/o/x, and then of women, this data proves the need for more programs, studies, outlets, spaces and mentoring for the Latina/o/x Hispanic student, faculty and staff at the university level, such as the CLWG.

I am reminded of a poem I wrote, *I am.,* (Medina De León, 2018) which I had begun to understand everything, every part of my life has affected my outlook, my identity, the many faceted aspects of what an identity is especially as a Chicana in academia facing a lack of representation on campus.

I am[2]

Finding identity,

my identity,
encompasses so much more
for me and the Indigenous identity…

…

I emulate those who are strong and wise,
but,
am not at all what you may think I should be.

What I am or what you think I should be, doesn't truly define me.
Because … I am more.

---

[1] Texas Tech University's Fact Book provides statistical demographic information including student enrollment, degrees awarded, faculty per program, etc.
[2] Excerpt of *I am*

I am learning... evolving.

I come from a richness of bold and strong women,
But find it hard as a Latina, a Mexican American woman,
to find the me within all that I already am and is expected of me.

...

And so, I am everything that I observe, that I love and admire
And that I would love to be, though I am not complete
In finding what it is that truly defines my identity.

INTENTIONS OF CLWG

The group began out of necessity. I have often stated that when I attended classes in college it was rare to "see myself," to find connections with those who had similar experiences. Throughout my experiences in academia, until more recently, it was difficult to find these "comadres,"—like-minded souls. We are often so compartmentalized that we do not see the importance of having a community amongst ourselves, like CLWG. A space, in existence, wherever and however that needs to form, as well as a space as a place. Research in studies among Latinas have stated, "since the beginning of time women have gathered at the well, the kitchen, the cradle, in fields, factories, and homes (Allende, 2020)," and "hallways, passages, kitchens, places in-between or outside of main events...these are the spaces of transit and possibility...where women actively created the space to have a separate Chicana platica" (Espinoza, et al., 2019). This is a space that I, nor my co-PI, at the time had privilege or access within the academic setting.

For a long time, I have been doing things on my own within this context of creating these "spaces." This is an important part of who I was, who I am, who I want to be remembered as, as vulnerable as it makes me. Vulnerability—is just that—putting yourself out there, mistakes, failures, successes—all of it—and being who you are, intentionally. I have learned, you must be resilient, you must persevere. Until one puts themselves out there, become vulnerable, but accepting of who they are, they will not find community. Being part of a community means you share and expose things about yourself yet feel safe enough to do so. In providing spaces/places, an actual place, a space of consciousness, a group, an organization, a class, etc., unless you can do that for yourself first, the people in those communities will not feel like they belong, like they are valued, that they and their issues do not matter.

Until I began taking courses in Women's and Gender Studies, WGS, spoke with new acquaintances, who had similar stories as mine.... until I lived every single part of my life, was I aware that I found a place/space/area where I feel more confident of my path/direction. Those who come to find these spaces would have resources (lived and learned experiences) available to them along with people, women, who had similar interests as them (Hurtado, 2020). As a Chicana/Latina in the academic arena, I see very little of my fellow Latinas at work. We are often swamped with advocating for ourselves, our positions, in our own realms within the university system. It is rare that we have the opportunity to sit and chat, having those conversations of what it means to be Latina in academia, at a predominately white institute, in areas, where we are very much the minority, and in areas where we and other people of underrepresented communities/identities are not considered when pedagogies, courses and such are built.

It is not uncommon that we as a gente attempt to forge a way for our future selves to have a space, reclaiming what was/is ours. There are countless studies on the importance of these spaces for Latinas in academia. For many, these spaces aide them in making sense of their identities among these types of communities—the processes (bodymindspirit cultivation and exchange of funds of knowledge), and communities of women's transformation—the holistic emotional corporal sense of self that Latinas carry (Ramirez, 2019).

In my privilege of being a Chicana/Latina tenured faculty member, although it has afforded me some things, such as a sense of job security, an adequate salary, funds for conferences, trainings, etc., I feel powerless and ambiguous. There are times it feels as though my words do not carry weight. Attempts of creating diverse spaces, such as CLWG, painstakingly making sure my intentions and goals align with those of the campus, have been, at times, met with a feeling of being pushed to the side and opposition. Other times, it is felt when making calls for diverse hires, for more diversity in our collections, or for the creation of special collections. There are times when I feel sabotaged, taken for granted, even attacked because of my identity, the things I stand for, and the service work I love. Though, through adversity, I take my position as a tenured faculty, with a funded working group, and utilize it to the advantage of helping others.

CLWG's goal and intention, onset, was stir dialogue on the influence of Chicana feminist thought and theory (Anzaldúa, 2021; Moraga, 1983). Because the university had attained HSI status, it was important to continue research and forge forward with dialogue, presence, and representation—not only in theory, but in our pedagogy, our curriculum, practices, and institutional climate. CLWG continues to find ways to integrate this consciousness into our everyday practices. Dedicated time to writing and working is another facet allowing engagement in a multitude of things: collaborating, brainstorming, writing, researching, practicing their teaching philosophy or presentations—an academic tamalada[3] or glorieta,[4] if you will (Castaneda et al., 2017; Hurtado, 2020). CLWG makes sure to allow for openness for community, inside and outside of the institution, and as such are open to all genders, gender queer or non-genders and any ethnicity or race.

---

[3] A tamalada is a gathering people uniting to make tamales and lessens the load of the principal preparer and provides a "space" where stories are shared. In Castañeda's (et.al) article, the term used is tamaleando - the process of working a tamalada.

[4] Hurtado defines a glorieta as spaces where people engage in dialogue with different audiences (32).

CLWG poses that Chicana/x Latina/x feminisms can influence work and research in an interdisciplinary/transdisciplinary way.

CLWG meets monthly, talks about any assigned reading(s), provides time for participants to work on their own work. Our members come together to collaborate, to create, to help each other and make lifelong connections—comadres. Comadrazgo, creating connections, is important among colleagues who are representative of BIPOC communities, who have similar experiences and who face similar challenges. It brings us closer together, creating a bond. Comadrazgo, an alliance of like-minded souls, in CLWG, Chicanas and Latinas, among other identities, coming together uniting in shared experiences mentoring and empowering each other (Ribero & Arellano, 2019)! According to Ribero and Arellano, as well as in other research, this type of mentoring framework works well among women of color, people of color, and with regards to CLWG, Latinas/Chicanas, because it is intersectional and accounts for the diverse lived experiences. It can help feminist scholars challenge models of feminism that reproduce universal ideas of women's experience (Espinoza et al., 2018; Ramirez, 2019; Ribero & Arellano, 2019).

CHICANA FEMINISMOS

There is necessity in building frameworks and pedagogy around Chicana Feminism. According to Aida Hurtado in *Intersectional Chicana Feminisms* and other works, Chicana feminism came into existence because of the lack of representation during the *Moviemiento* and inequalities that were/are not addressed in other feminisms, with an emphasis on Mexican and Chicana/o/x culture, history, language, oppression, etc. (Hurtado, 2020). Chicana Feminism also fights against the cultural tax that is placed upon us—as in Anzaldúa teoría of mestizaje, that we are not just a single identity, but carry multiple identities (Anzaldúa, 2021; Hurtado, 2020). In academia, for example, I at times, wear many hats, even at my own volition. As a woman of color, a Latina, I have had to serve multiple times on search committees—making the committee diverse in representation. Sometimes filling this capacity negates the need to add other BIPOC representatives, especially if there are no seats to be filled. Other times, I serve on committees across campus thinking, with the mindset of the inclusion of all entities involved BIPOC and underserved identities, as the library representative. Let us not disregard the familial and societal implications—how we as Latinas/Chicanas are viewed, whether our lenguaje is up to par, if we are applauded or thought of as "que se cree mucho" (Anzaldúa, 2021; Hurtado, 2020).

CHICANA/LATINA/" & THE 'X

Chicana refers to Mexican American descent, it has several iterations of meanings and context, from being a dirty word, implications of political and radicalization. The Chicano Movement of the 60s and 70s, and from what we, as a working group refer to, a more holistic meaning to include every aspect of our culture and heritage, to name/label ourselves. Key texts and research that CLWG utilizes are/were created by Chicana feminists as well. The 'x' significa inclusion of all genders. However, the use of labels, although important, is not what the focus is. In the spirit of this chapter and the call for comadrazgo, we are here in this space to support one another, lift one another up, for whatever each person needs at the moment in this space.

We utilized the platform to introduce various literature to the group, having discussions based loosely on works by Cherrie Moraga and Gloria Anzaldúa—*This Bridge Called My Back* and *Borderlands/La Frontera* (Anzaldúa, 2021; Moraga, 1983). As time progressed, more literature was incorporated into many sessions including poetry, readings, articles, and other works that were and are integral to CLWG goals. These works included *Chicana Movidas* edited by Dionne Espinoza et al. (2018); Gloria Anzaldúa's "Border Arte: Neplanta, El Lugar de la Frontera" in Hernandez-Avila and Cantú's *Entre Guadalupe y Malinche* (2016); Anzaldúa's "To Live in the Borderlands Means You" and "Don't Give In, Chicanita" in *Borderlands/La Frontera* (2021). We also included Cherrie Moraga's *Native Country of the Heart* (2019); and Gaspar de Alba's [Un]Framing the "Bad Woman (2014)." Corina and I received opportunities for speaking engagements through at TTU's WGS program. In Fall of 2019, we participated in TTU's WGS Feminist First Friday speaking to participants regarding Chicana feminism and aided them in creating a zine that spoke to Chicana feminism and art and invited to attend and speak during a graduate seminar course specifically regarding Chicana Feminisms. We created, moderated, and participated in a panel that was presented at TTU's 5th Annual Hispanic/Latinx Research & Creativity Symposium hosted by the College of Media & Communication in March 2020. The panel consisted of 4 of our group members, and discussed 1) identifying as a Chicana, or with Chicanas, and or Chicana Feminism; 2) Belonging to and the significance of the Chicana/x Latina/x working Group and 3) importance of the working group and/or Chicana Feminism in their research /discipline.

The COVID-19 pandemic took its toll on our members and in retrospect proved that the group's existence mattered. Many of our members felt isolated during Lubbock's stay-at-home order making them feel the absence of others, missed conversations that organically come about the office, not knowing what and how everyone they had come to be in a space/place with was. We met virtually and talked of plans, of how we were doing, and sometimes nothing. Some members also dealt with personal and work matters. The group needed to be more fluid, really be a space, much more in the abstract than physical, and be used however it was needed—being open to more possibilities. For example, because of the ongoing risk for Covid and accessibility of Zoom, recent events were created to meet those needs. One such event was the "Conversations with CLWG" in the Spring 2022. We invited a panel of artists and discussed their artwork and the space that they created. This time the event was more of a venue for other Latinas/Chicanas to use as a platform to showcase the work they created. Another

"Conversations w/CLWG," also held in Spring 2022, focused on *Jefas*[5] and featured Latinas/Chicanas in the community who have made those boss moves to accomplish their goals. This space was also a platform for an exhibit as well as a Latina owned jewelry pop-up shop. CLWG's space provided support for these three projects. One of our first presentations when we returned from quarantine was a presentation at REFORMA's[6] National Conference in October 2021. Our goal was to spread word of CLWG, our initiatives, and inspire others to achieve similar feats at their institution. We planted the seed—being intentional the need for and creation of "claiming/reclaiming space" for the Latinx community. We also proposed future collaborations with these groups. We were received well, and I even began mentoring a new librarian who was in a similar situation as I, the only Latina at her library. Having this "space," the participants agreed, was an overall good thing and few mentioned they wished they had these types of groups.

CLWG ASPIRATIONS

Since Covid and the return to somewhat normalcy on campus, CLWG's funding was extended for another year. As stated, we are exploring innovative ways to claim/reclaim "space" for our members and the community and provide CLWG services outside of research and writing. We hope to renew our proposal to include updated goals that focus on pedagogy of learned and lived experience(s) as important facets (Delgado Bernal, 2006). We acknowledge that we should make sure to include TTU staff in our plans, as staff do not always have the flexibility that faculty may have. We have been discussing possibilities of collaborating with the libraries' MakerSpace and creating workshops that will provide opportunities to create. Ideally, I would like to take CLWG to another level and establish an actualized center within TTU's Institute for [Mexican American and Latino Studies AND Latin American and Iberian Studies][7] that focuses on Chicana/Latina feminism and serves as a space conducive to those needing this space for various learning, research, and collaborating.

Faculty, staff, and students and those in the community, especially BIPOC populations, need spaces like these. In the past and presently, these spaces provide an opportunity for building connections, mentoring each other, representing our culture, to help and support one another. These spaces are not always provided for us, and we must claim or reclaim them making sure that what we do, who we are, what we want to say is seen and heard. Finally, I share an excerpt from one of my poems, *"Sopita de Letras,"* written during the fall 2021 Women's and Gender Studies Women of Color class.

---

[5] *Jefas*, translated, are women in charge, boss women.
[6] REFORMA—National Association to Promote Library & Information Services to Latinos and the Spanish Speaking.
[7] The TTU Institute for Mexican American and Latino Studies AND Latin American and Iberian Studies has not been officially named..

"They" told me
that if I wanted to be a leader
that I should look for another line of work...
be someone else...
not in those words of course

it was fuel
added to my fire

squeaking by because no one told me
taught me
what it was really like

first-gen in everything that I do,
no matter the level, the higher in academia I get
FIRST-GEN meaning everything that I do is learned/will be learned
however it is that I learn it
because there was/is nothing out there in my proximity
until more recently

squeaking by,
utilizing my positionality
using myself as a platform
regardless of tokenism
for others to use
not always ideal
but useful in situaciones where others
that LOOK como yo
que necessitan una espacio un lugar

TO BE

un lugar solo para ellos nosotros ustedes y yo...

REFERENCES

Anzaldúa, G. (2016). Border Arte: Neplanta, el lugar de la frontera [Border Art: Neplanta, the place of the border]. In I. Hernandez-Avila & N. E. Cantú (Eds.), *Entre Guadalupe y Malinche: Tejanas in literature and art* .[In between Guadalupe and Malinche: Texas women in literature and art] (pp. 23–32). University of Texas Press.

Anzaldúa, G. (2021). *Borderlands/La Frontera: The new mestiza* (R. Vivancos-Pérez & N. E. Cantú, Eds.). Aunt Lute Books. (Original work published 1987)

Castañeda, M., Anguiano, A. A., & Alemán, D. M. (2017). Voicing for space in academia: Testimonios of Chicana communication professors. *Chicana/Latina Studies, 16*(2), 158–188.

Delgado Bernal, D., Elenes, C. A., Godinez, F. E., & Villenas, S. (Eds.). (2006). *Chicana/Latina education in everyday life: Feminista perspectives on pedagogy and epistemology*. New York Press.

Division of Diversity Equity & Inclusion. (2021, March 30). *Hispanic serving institution.* https://www.depts.ttu.edu/diversity/institutional-diversity/hispanic-serving/
Espinoza, D., Cotera, M. E., & Blackwell, M. (Eds.). (2018). *Chicana movidas: New narratives of activism and feminism in the movement era.* University of Texas Press.
Gaspar de Alba, A. (Ed.). (2014). *[Un]framing the "bad woman": Sor Juana, Malinche, Coyolxauhqui and other rebels with a cause.* University of Texas Press.
Hurtado, A. (2020). *Intersectional Chicana feminisms: Sitios y lenguas.* The University of Arizona Press.
Martinez, E. I. (2020). *A jaguar in the library: The story of the first Chicana librarian.* Floricanto Press.
Medina De León, E. (2018). *I am.* Poetry.
Medina De León, E. (2022). *Sopita de Letras.* Poetry. https://estmed77.wixsite.com/latinalibrarian/post/sopita-de-letras-abcs-let-me-spell-it-out-for-you
Moraga, C. (2019). *Native country of the heart : a memoir* (1st ed.). Farrar, Straus and Giroux.
Moraga, C., & Anzaldúa, G. (1983). *This bridge called my back: Writings by radical women of color* (2nd ed.). Kitchen Table, Women of Color Press.
Ramirez, J. J. (2019). *Cultivando y transformando: Communities of women among Latinas in academia* (Publication No. 13885339) [Doctoral dissertation, University of Pittsburgh}. ProQuest Dissertations Publishing.
Ribero, A.M., & Arellano, S.C. (2019). Advocating *comandrismo*: A feminist mentoring approach for Latinas in rhetoric and composition. *Peitho Journal, 21*(2), 334–356.
Texas Tech University Institutional Research. (2022, April 29). *TTU fact book.* http://techdata.irs.ttu.edu/FactBook/Enrollment/ENRETHNIC.aspx Accessed 2/28/2022.
Wiggins, L. (2018). "Women need to find their voice": Latinas speak out in the Midwest, 1972. In Espinoza, D., Cotera, M. E., & Blackwell, M. (Eds.), *Chicana movidas: New narratives of activism and feminism in the movement era* (pp. 76–90). University of Texas Press.

CHAPTER 3

VISUAL TESTIMONIOS

Artist/Writer Acts of Resistance and Recovery

Christen Sperry García
University of Texas Rio Grande Valley

Leslie C. Sotomayor II
Texas Tech University

Alexis Marie Ramos
South Texas College

Elizabeth Gonzalez, Ricky Sullivan, Lourdes Garcia, Adilene Rosales, Rocio Guerrero, Mandy Wilson, and Nydia Salinas
University of Texas Rio Grande Valley

Visual testimonios are a performative practice of nepantla, a creative act of living in-between worlds (Sotomayor & García, 2022). We theorize through performing image and text. A residue of the act of nepantla, we make our stories visual. Gloria Anzaldúa (1999, 2009, 2012) emphasizes that our stories, testimonios, autohistorias are performances—a collaborative effort between the reader and writer, and/or artist. Using a visual language to share one's testimonio, the artist/writer engages in autohistoria-teoría, theorizing through lived experience. This visual/performance text is a result of a workshop that guided artist/writers through a nine-step reflection process.

Visual testimonios are a performative practice of nepantla, a creative act of living in-between worlds (Sotomayor & García, 2022). We theorize through performing image and text. A residue of the act of nepantla, we make our stories visual. Gloria Anzaldúa (1999, 2009, 2012) emphasizes that our stories, testimonios, autohistorias are performances—a collaborative effort between the reader and writer, and/or artist. Writing performatively is a feminist/artist/act—an embodiment of the self through visual text. Visual testimonios are a feminist methodology of decolonizing the self and bodies of knowledge. Using a visual language to share one's testimonio, the artist/writer engages in autohistoria-teoría, theorizing through lived experience. Through a collaging of image and text, the maker/performer navigates tense, ambiguous, and shifting borderlands spaces.

A decolonizing act, visual testimonios do not follow traditional academic writing guidelines. For example, we do not italicize non-English words. Through translanguaging, we use two or more languages together and recognize that language identities are plural and embodied acts (García & Wei, 2014). An act of transcultural recovery, we recover what has been lost or repressed through colonization (Montoya, 2021). As curadoras (healer/curator), we occupy multiple spaces critically while acknowledging fluid intersections toward new knowledge creation and transformation. While our Spanish may not be spelled in the same way as colloquial Spanish, we often spell as we pronounce these words as English was taught in our schools over Spanish.

Visual testimonios are a process of simultaneous fragmentation and wholeness. Coyolxauhqui is an Aztec warrior goddess of the moon who was sacrificed and dismembered by Huitzilopochtli, the god of war, in Aztec mythology way. Anzaldúa and Keating (2015) refer to Coyolxauhqui as one who represents "the psychic and creative process of tearing apart and pulling together. She represents fragmentation, imperfection, incompleteness, and unfulfilled promises, as well as integration, completeness, and wholeness" (p. 50). To live and work with Coyolxauhqui, the visual testimonio maker becomes comfortable with the uncomfortable: disruption, fragmentation, and the process of becoming whole in a new way.

The below visual testimonios came out of a workshop with MFA artist/writers at The University Texas Rio Grande Valley School of Art and Design. Artist/writers were guided through a nine-step reflection process.

- **Curadora:** What experience has changed you in some way?
- **Nepantla**: How do you find yourself living between two worlds?
- **Teorizar/theorize**: How does nepantla relate to your lived experiences?
- **Autohistoria**: Create a .docx file to tell your story
- **Decolonize**: Do not write in academic paragraph form
- **Visualize**: Include images alone, no captions or figures
- **Coyolxauhqui**: Write in fragmented thoughts
- **Translanguage**: Use two or more languages/dialects simultaneously
- **Collectivity:** Share your visual testimon

OLD 83

"Cuando me muera, quiero que le agan Cazo a su papa"
:"ay, ama no se va morir"!!!

Es nadamas un sueno....   PORQUE NOSOTROS????

☹ Denial   😢 Sadness   😠 Anger

trying me best....

Goal #1: Be the first in my family to graduate from H.S

Older Sisters: "No digas eso, es lo Que dijimos todas y miranos"

"LA GRADUADA" 🎓 HS

When are you getting married??? Se te va pasar el tren 🚂   Como llegue aqui?

PARTY!!!!WORK!!!SCHOOL.... REPEAT

"LA GRADUADA" 🎓 **MASSAGE THERAPY**
"LA GRADUADA" 🎓 **ASSOCIATES GRAPHIC DESIGN**

LIFE   IM OK!

"LA GRADUADA" 🎓 **BACHELORS IN STUDIO ART/MINOR PSYCHOLOGY**

FREEDOM   LA vida da *muchas* vueltas
Nunca te vemos....we miss you
Adilene Rosales   **"GRAD DEGREE COMING SOON"** 🎓

xxxxxxxxxxxxxxxxxxxxxxxxxxx　　　　　　　　xxxxxxxxxxxxxxxxxxxxxxxxxxxxxxxx

••••••••••••••••••••••• The color of my skin. ••
|||||| Which a mirror cannot hide. ||||||||||||||||||||||||||||||||||||||||
ΔΔΔΔΔΔΔΔΔΔΔΔΔΔΔΔΔΔΔΔΔΔΔΔΔΔΔΔΔΔΔΔΔΔΔΔΔΔΔΔΔΔΔΔ An issue I have dealt with since a child.
///
◊◊◊◊◊◊◊◊◊◊◊◊◊◊◊◊◊◊◊◊◊◊◊◊◊◊◊◊◊◊◊

La Morena. ◊◊◊◊◊◊◊◊◊◊◊◊◊◊◊◊◊◊◊◊◊◊◊◊◊◊◊◊◊
::::::::::::::::::: La Negra. ::
〰〰〰　〰〰〰　〰〰〰　〰〰〰　Even at times a derogatory word.　〰〰〰〰〰〰〰　〰〰
;;;;;;;;;;;;
Was I to embrace? ::::::::::::::::::::::::::
""""""""""""""""""""""""""""""""""""" This system of love. """"""""""""""""""
～～～　A love I could not comprehend.　～～～
Xxxxxxxxxxxxxxxxxxxxxxxxx xxxxxxxxxxxxxxxxxxx xxxxxxxxxxx This type of love made no sense.
<<<<<<<<<<<<<<>>>>>>>>>>>>>>>

################## ##### I see that girl in the mirror. ########### ######### ###########
The morenita. ((((((((((((((((((((((((((((((((((()))))))))))))))))))))))
{{{{{{{{{{{{{{{{{{{{{{{{{{{{{{{{{{{{{}}}}}}}}}}}}}}}}}}}}}}}}}}}}}}}}}} Jugando.
[[[[[[[[[[[[[[[]]]]]]]]]]]]]]] Aciendo, pos niña. [[[[[[[[[[[[[[[[[[[[[[[[[[[[[]]]]]]]]]]]]]]]]]]]]]
?????????????????????????
Scars that grew. ....
.... Wounds to heal. ....
.... Who has decided to view my skin,
And discriminate. ɔɔɔɔɔɔɔɔɔɔ ɔɔɔɔɔɔɔɔɔɔɔɔɔ   ɔɔɔɔɔɔɔɔɔɔɔɔɔɔɔɔɔɔɔɔɔɔɔɔɔ ɔɔɔɔɔɔɔɔ ɔɔɔɔɔɔɔ
++

«««««««««««««« Soy mujer. ««««««««««««««««««
.... Soy Morena.
Embrace. ||||||||||||||||||||||||||||||||||||||||||||||||||||||||||||||
************************* Si. ****************
+++++++++++++++++++++++++++++++++++ Por que no.
000000000000

Elizabeth Gonzalez

empty, dark, shallow life...

But **God**, light, joy, forgiveness

Life changes...

TRANSPLANTED To TEXAS, FUNNY LOUISIANA ACCENT GRADUALLY DISAPPEARS HILL COUNTRY, RIVERS, FRIENDS

Marriage ++

1+1= Children born

Beautiful
Tender
Love
Hold
Feed
Hug

Life changes...

TRANSPLANTED To EDINBURG, LONELY, HOT, JOBLESS, GRADUALLY DISAPPEARS COOL BEACHES, YELLOW SUNFLOWERS, PRETTY PALM TREES, FRIENDS

KIDS

growing Laughing

Fun   HOTCOCOA   Fuzzy Slippers

Family life

Mandy Wilson

I found it   *Tan Chiquitita*   Y sin querer la perdi   En casa de mi madre   Very
angry face

!!!!!!!!!!!!!!!!!!

!!   .....   !!

!!   ::::::   !!

!!   ::::::   !!

?   ::::   ?

-Te pareces mucho a tu padre

Pobre…

siempre enojado-

Reflexiones, reflexiones, reflexiones...

Z   !!!!!   Z

Z   !!!!!!!!! Z

Z   !!!!!!!! Z

Z   @@   Z

ZZZZZZZZZZZ

Very short visit   *Y de regreso a casa*   *Inner child discovered*
…tarea que hacer

Las cosas cambian, y una tan testaruda.

Quiereme mucho, cuidame y dime que todo va a estar bien.

No es tu culpa… ni de nadie. Asi es la vida, a veces. No mas culpas. No more guilt.

Become exactly what you want to be.   **Freedom.**   *Be happy and count your blessings.* -*Ya comprenderas cuando seas madre.* She does not say- I told you- *You are the first in my heart.*   *Y no lo sabes.*   *O si*

Lourdes Garcia

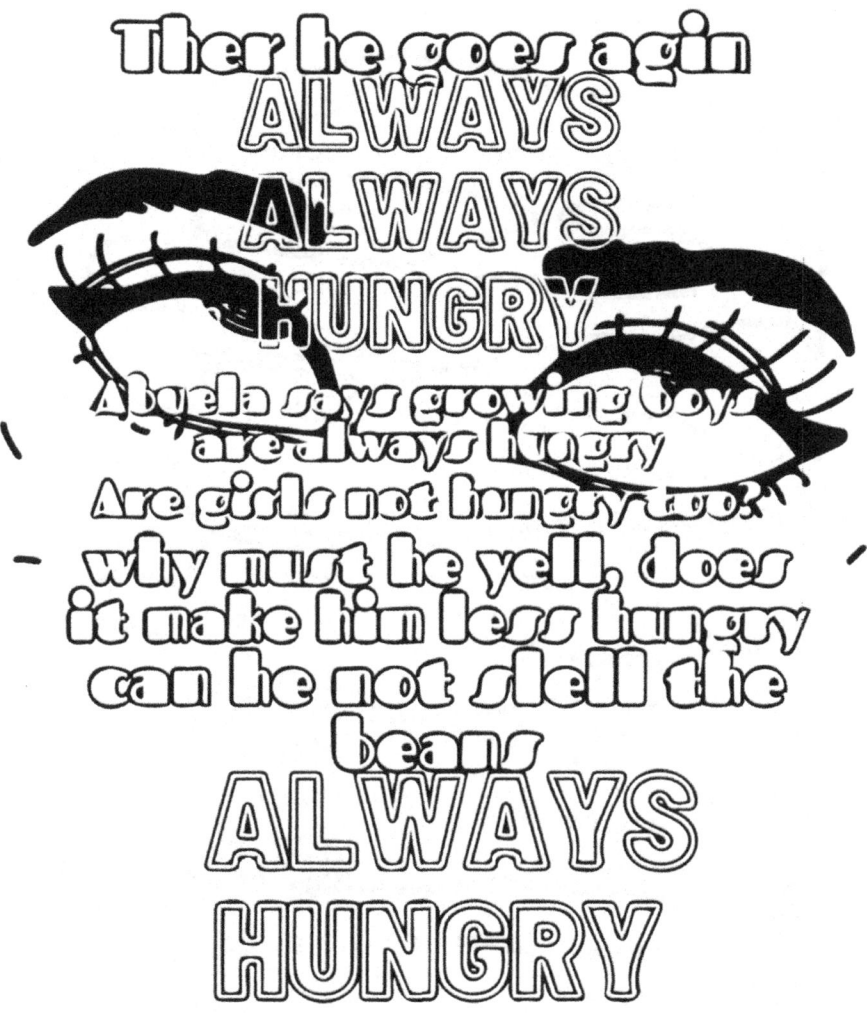

Alexis Ramos

Mujer Fuerte

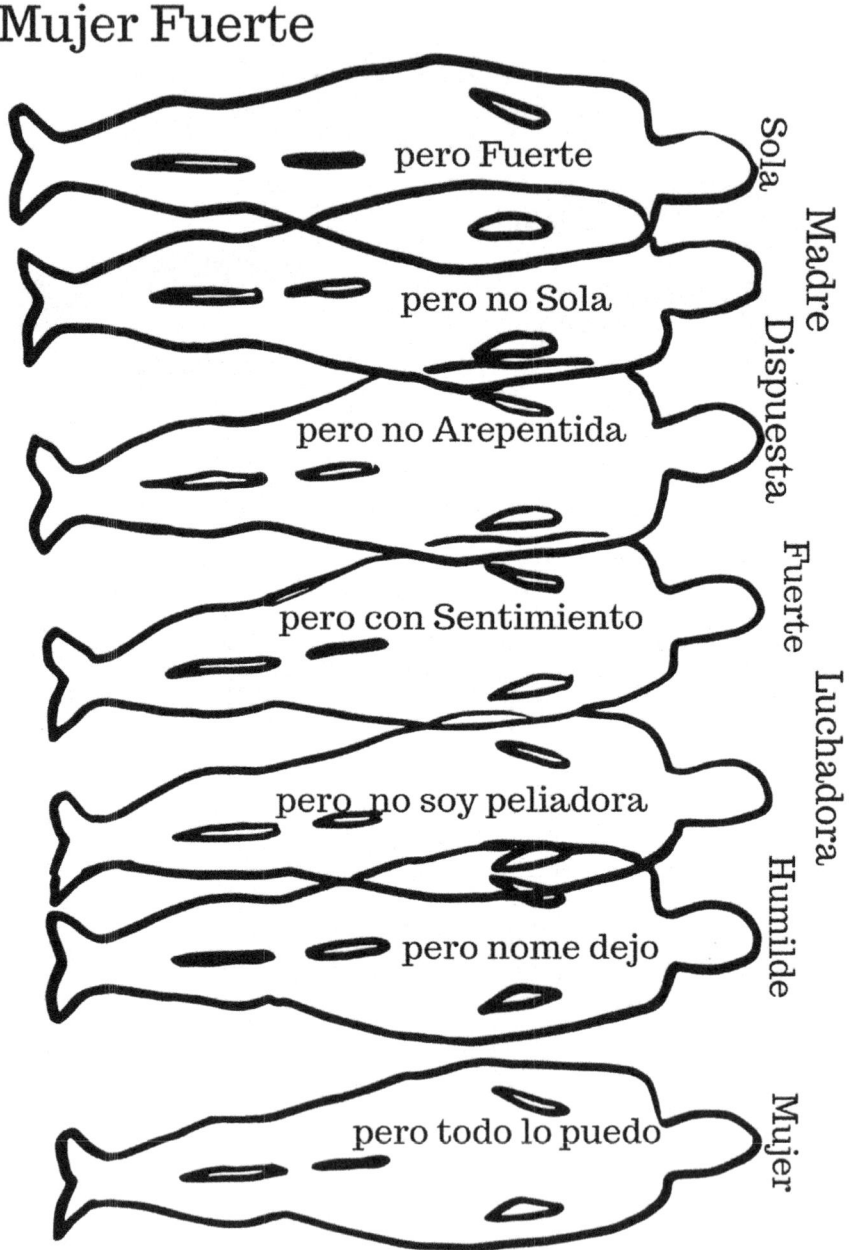

Rocio Guerrero

Ricky Sullivan

REFERENCES

Anzaldúa, G. (1999). *Borderlands: La frontera: The new mestiza* (2nd ed.). Aunt Lute Books.
Anzaldúa, G. (2012). *Borderlands/la frontera: The new mestiza*, 4th ed. Aunt Lute Books.
Anzaldúa, G., & Keating, A. (2009). *The Gloria Anzaldúa reader.* Duke University Press.
Anzaldúa, G., & Keating, A. (2015). *Luz en lo oscuro: Rewriting identity, spirituality, reality.* Duke University Press.
García, O., & Wei, L., (2014). *Translanguaging: Language, bilingualism and education.* Palgrave Macmillan.
Montoya, A. (2021). Intersectionality, liminal space: A teacher's testimonio using testimonios in a writing college class. In J. Jupp (Chair), *Decolonial options in critical curricular-pedagogical praxis: Testimonios de aprendizaje in transnational context.* Curriculum & Pedagogy Group 22nd Annual Conference.
Sotomayor, L. C., & García, C. S. (2022). Visual testimonios: Acts of healing and resistance. In A. Miles de Perez & K. Jenkins (Chairs) *Women's caucus business meeting I: Latina/x and Chicana/x Art & pedagogy*. The National Art Education Association (NAEA) Conference. NYC.

CHAPTER 4

HOME, FAMILY, AND HISTORY

Highlighting an Underrepresented Geographic And Cultural Narrative

Gina Gwen Palacios
University of Texas Rio Grande Valley

Drawing on my family history and Mexican American identity, I use paint, cardboard, cotton, and other materials to create artwork of an often underrepresented geographic and cultural narrative. My name is Gina Gwen Palacios and I'm an artist and professor from South Texas. Growing up, I absorbed my parents' stories about cotton picking, migrant farm work, and the discrimination they experienced in the region, including being punished for speaking Spanish, having their first names anglicized, and being forced out of school. Although vast expanses of the southwestern United States were once part of Mexico, Mexican American families who have deep roots in the area are often treated as outsiders, as usurpers of the land and resources their families have occupied, in many cases, for generations. Below, I share 8 visual testimonios, artwork representing my individual perspective which, in turn, represents the larger collective story (Blackmer Reyes & Curry Rodríguez, 2012) of my family and the history of many Tejanos. I use colors and materials that emphasize the connection to our surroundings and the long cultural lineage of which I am a part.

FIGURE 4.1. Gina Gwen Palacios, Hermana y Hermano, 2018. Cotton, charcoal, acrylic, and hand carved cardboard. 29 ½ x 22 ½".

In *Hermana y Hermano* (Figure 4.1) I recreated a photo of my father and tía. Their clothing was replaced with the cotton they would have picked, and their skin is made up of and matches the color of cardboard and vegetable boxes that they filled. I started working with cardboard because it is a material that is everywhere, it's useful and strong, yet fragile and disposable. I saw a similarity between our dependence on cardboard and the labor of many Mexican Americans. America is so dependent on this labor, yet many are made to feel expendable.

FIGURE 4.2. Gina Gwen Palacios, "*Cotton-Pickin*," 2018. Wood, hand carved cardboard, stand oil, and sandpaper. 76 x 44".

FIGURE 4.3. Gina Gwen Palacios, *Josefina*, 2017. Oil on panel. 6 x 6".

In the work, "*Cotton-Pickin*" (Figure 4.2), I highlight the people and slogan of my hometown of Taft, Texas. In my parents' youth, train tracks separated the laborers from the white landowners. Considering the history of segregation and racism in this small town, the slogan "Friendliest Cotton Pickin' Town in Texas" takes on a new meaning. The work was created to represent a billboard that sits at the town's edge. The figures are made up of hand carved cardboard, their skin is represented by sandpaper, and their hair is stained by oil. This work is based off a photo of my grandmother, father, and tía, three of the countless unknown laborers who helped build what America is today.

FIGURE 4.4. Gina Gwen Palacios, *American Primitive*, 2017. Oil on canvas. 44 x 60".

FIGURE 4.5. Gina Gwen Palacios, *Pienso En Ti*, 2017. Acrylic on mylar. 39 x 35".

American Primitive (Figure 4.4) represents my family history and that of many Tejanos of South Texas. It includes the flat horizon line, a wide-open sky, the picking fields, and familia. This mother and son lived on the borderlands of the Rio Grande Valley. The woman is darker than her son whose hand she holds. Maybe

FIGURE 4.6. Gina Gwen Palacios, *Burial at Edinburg (Death of a Cotton Picker)*, 2017. Oil on canvas. 10 x 11".

she has more indigenous features than him or she's *quemada* from picking in the sun every day. One day, her son, who will pick by her side, will be as dark as she is. Both of their skin tones match the color of the brown earth beneath them. The growing cotton fields are there, far in the distance, but still present, a generational memory and history that continues to impact the proceeding generations. For me, *American Primitive, Josefina* (Figure 4.3), and *Cabbage and Watermelons* (Figure 4.7) represent the humble beginnings of the American Dream. I view these works as American paintings, *American Primitive* as my own version of Grant Wood's, *American Gothic* (1930). These works sit in the vein of social realism and portrayals of the heroic working class, but I think of them more as frontera or border realism.

In Jennifer González's book *Subject to Display: Reframing Race in Contemporary Installation Art* (2008) González describes *autotopography* as a mix of autobiography, history, and current events used to emphasize personal experience as situated within a particular time. *Pienso En Ti* (Figure 4.5) is a large-scale reinterpretation of a Mexican handmade object created specifically for a loved one. Time, space, and event collapse and are embedded in these stitched artifacts which come in many forms, like hand towels and pillows. These autotopographical objects become a physical map of history, memory, and a replacement for the intangible aspects of identity and social relations.

Dientes Afuera (Figure 4.8) was both a common saying and a strategy for survival for many Mexican Americans. In responding to the racism and misogyny

FIGURE 4.7.   Gina Gwen Palacios, *Cabbage & Watermelons*, 2017. Oil on panel. 6 x 6".

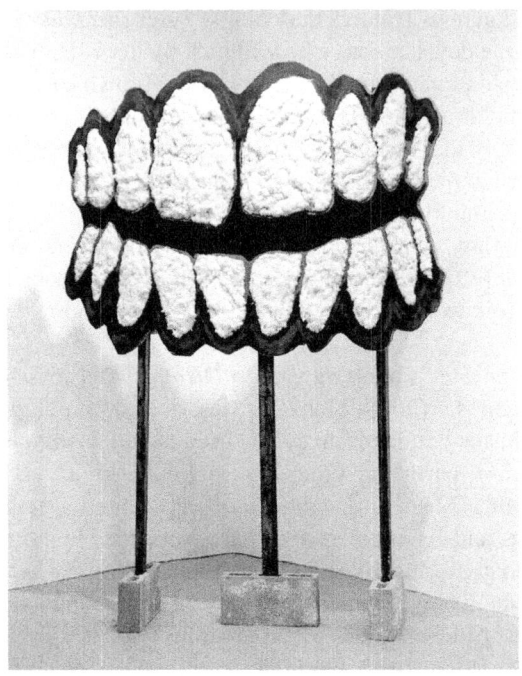

FIGURE 4.8. Gina Gwen Palacios, *Dientes Afuera*, 2018. Cardboard, acrylic, cotton, pumice, wood, and cement. 88 x 64".

my mother faced, she sought safety in silence, albeit through gritted teeth. She passed on this mantra of *dientes afuera*, which translates to "teeth outside" or was understood to me as "just smile and hold your tongue." This large, billboard style work is a recreation of my teeth, assembled using cardboard, cotton, and oil, holding the carved-out words "dientes afuera" between them. Charcoal and pumice (grit) sit in the space between the teeth and on top of the text. I carry that mantra's weight and its contradictions—the expectation of 'smile and survive' existing in tension with a need to speak up, or to scream.

REFERENCES

Blackmer Reyes, K., & Curry Rodríguez, J. (2012). Testimonio: Origins, terms, and resources. *Equity & Excellence in Education, 45*(3), 525–538.

González, J. (2008). *Subject to display: Reframing race in contemporary installation art*. MIT Press.

CHAPTER 5

A CHICANO-ISH, CHICANO, CHICAN@, OR CHICANX ARTIST STATEMENT

Paul Valadez
University of Texas Rio Grande Valley

Spanish was my father's first language, but in school he was not allowed to speak it. My grandparents, especially my grandmother, did not speak much English. My father did not want his boys to have the trouble he had in school, so my brother and I never learned to speak Spanish. Spanish was the language of mysteries to me, things I was not supposed to know as a child. Decades later, I tried to join a "Mexican-American" club in art school, I was not allowed to enter and was voted out because I did not speak Spanish. For years I have been fascinated by language. This fascination has informed much of my artwork in letterforms, fragmented language, misspellings, and Spanish text.

In the last decade or so my artwork has dealt with decolonization and identity. My father's experience of being forced not to speak Spanish is an example of colonization. Contrasting this to my experience, my individual identity of not being Mexican enough if I did not speak Spanish is at the core of the Chicano movement and this idea of identity. I think it is the common experiences shared by a group that define its people, not skin color, last name, or religion. To me, the most common experience is food. There has NEVER been a time in my life when I was not

FIGURE 5.1. Paul Valadez, untitled, Acrylic on Canvas, 16 x 20 in, 2022.

FIGURE 5.2. Paul Valadez, untitled, acrylic on canvas, 16 x 20 in, 2022

A Chicano-ish, Chicano, Chican@, or ChicanX Artist Statement • 45

FIGURE 5.3. Paul Valadez, untitled, acrylic on cardboard, 12 x 36 in, 2022

served Mexican food. I distinctly remember the first time I had Japanese food, but I always had Mexican food. I particularly remember the first time I had Japanese food, but I always had Mexican food. My current artwork is about Mexican food, and explore through graphic images, and embraces the decolonization; the idea of rejecting the ideals of the dominant culture, of food through imagery.

FIGURE 5.4. Paul Valadez, untitled, acrylic on found advertisement, 30 x 40 in, 2020.

CHAPTER 6

(RE)MEMBERING, (RE)CONSTRUCTING, AND (RE)IMAGINING EXPERIENCE

Decolonizing Epistemological and Ontological Assumptions Formed in the Academy Through the Use of Autohistoria-Teoría in the Classroom

Kristin Alder
Texas Tech University

I recount the experience of using autohistoria-teoria in an undergraduate women's and gender studies course largely populated with women of color and/or queer students. Through the writing of autohistoria-teorias, some of which I will share, the students claimed identities and made sense of experiences, connected personal experience to social narratives, exposed the limitations of existing paradigms and canonized exemplars of feminist theory and practice, and fostered individual and collective healing and growth. Moreover, utilized in a classroom of students who often find themselves alienated from and invalidated by the academy, the autohistoria-teorías as social justice praxis, serve as forms of sociopolitical resistance which can disrupt academic canons and decolonize epistemological and ontological assumptions formed in the academy.

Gloria E. Anzaldúa uses the term "autohistoria-teoría" throughout her work to describe a theory and a method of autobiographical narrative that blends personal and cultural biographies with myth, storytelling, history, and other forms of theorizing. Through the composition of autohistoria-teorías, writers seek personal and cultural understanding that can ultimately be employed in social justice work. Personal memoir becomes a lens through which to better understand cultural narratives and how these cultural stories can be reread and rewritten to promote healing, self-growth, cultural critique, and individual and collective transformation. I employ autohistoria-teoría in my women's and gender studies (WGS) classrooms as a methodology and epistemology that not only fosters an engagement with feminist theories, but additionally cultivates knowledge creation, meaning, and identity through self-inscription, while blurring the boundaries between private and public borders and ultimately decolonizing traditional ways of theorizing about knowledge in the academy.

In this chapter, I recount the experience of using autohistoría-teoria as a white professor in an undergraduate capstone course in WGS largely populated with women of color and/or queer students at a Texas public university. As a group, these students expressed their desire to become more knowledgeable about feminist theory, but simultaneously spoke of the ways in which some theories they had engaged with in other courses had left them feeling alienated by and disconnected from the feminist movement. In elucidation, the students explained that much of the theory they had encountered did not speak to their experiences as women of color and/or queer persons. In what follows, I share how Anzaldúa's own theories and writings served as vehicles for student discovery, sources of inspiration, and additionally, subverted hesitation about the importance of lived experience in the classroom. Through the writing of autohistoría-teorias, some of which I will share, the students claimed identities and made sense of experiences, connected personal experience to social narratives, exposed the limitations of existing paradigms and canonized exemplars of feminist theory and practice, and fostered individual and collective healing and growth. Moreover, utilized in a classroom of predominantly BIPOC and queer students who often find themselves alienated from and invalidated by the academy, the autohistoría-teorías as social justice praxis, serve as forms of sociopolitical resistance which can disrupt academic canons and decolonize epistemological and ontological assumptions formed in the academy.

One critical goal of the course for me, as the instructor, was to encourage my students to consider what it meant to live a feminist life. With this goal in mind, I asked my students to think deeply about their definition of feminism, how and why feminism became a part of their lives, and what impact they wished feminism to have upon their life moving forward. Their autohistoria-teorías, then, explored their own life experiences and the histories of their development as feminists. Further, I directed students to consider how their own social location (their race, ethnicity, sex, gender, class, sexuality, and/or disability, etc.) influenced this overall discussion.

To inspire the students, I utilized Anzaldúa's path of conocimiento as a framework and a methodology for (re)membering, (re)constructing, and even (re)imagining experience. The path of conocimiento, detailed in her chapter "now let us shift... the path of conocimiento... inner work, public acts," is a spiritual, psychological, intellectual, and even embodied journey that enhances self-reflexivity and self-awareness that offers a way to understand the world, the self, and the role of the self in the world. It is a journey towards understanding and awareness, or conocimiento. Anzaldúa divides the path of conocimiento into seven recursive processes: el arrebato, nepantla, the Coatlicue state, the call, putting Coyolxauhqui together, a clash of realities, and spiritual activism. As one engages in the interdependent stages, one gains a complexity of knowledge about the self and the world that deepens one's understanding and perceptions of relationality. Moreover, the path of conocimiento is not a process where one merely graduates from one step and moves on to the next. The process is much more complicated. Oftentimes, one may find themselves not only in one step of the process, but in two or three simultaneously. The steps do not form a hierarchical relationship from one to seven but lay on top of one another. And, between and during most steps, there is almost always the second step, nepantla.

Early on in the semester, students were required to read and discuss Anzaldúa's piece, "now let us shift." To think more broadly about how Anzaldúa's path of conocimiento might help them better understand themselves and their worlds, I assigned various writing and small group discussions which provided the opportunity to reflect and compose. These activities created multidimensional opportunities for self-reflection and highlighted the importance of autohistoria-teoría as a space for both personal and collective growth. As the students shared and helped each other make sense of experience, their writing took on a communal quality in that each individual autohistoria-teoría became interwoven with the insight of their peers. Moreover, as students postulated about what they would have done had they been in the writer's position, writers were encouraged to embrace the imaginal potential of autohistoria-teoría in the understanding that fiction, too, informs our understanding of self and the world.

THE AUTOHISTORIA-TEORÍAS

Before I continue, a note about the use of student work throughout this chapter: To ensure their privacy, I have not attached the students' names to their work. I have chosen to use phrases like "one student" or "one young woman." In aligning the students' work with the various steps of the path of conocimiento, I have used the students' own thoughts and conclusions about their work versus imposed my own judgements. That the assignment called for their reflection in this way, added to their overall understanding of Anzaldúa's work, as well as their ability to make sense of their own experience. I have occasionally had to edit the students' work for length. Aside from this, their pieces appear as they were written by the students.

El Arrebato

The journey towards heightened consciousness on the path of conocimiento begins with "el arrebato," or a "rupture," that shakes you awake figuratively and perhaps literally, knocking you from your mental and physical stupor (Anzaldúa, 2002, p. 544). Students were inspired to consider whether there were moments that shocked them into (re)considering their view of themselves and/or their community. One student (re)constructed her el arrebato moment, writing:

> One day I was sitting on the couch and my mother came up to me and asked me to hand her my phone, it was then that she found out her daughter was a lesbian. I will never forget the words that my mother said to me that night. *"Como puedes hacernos esto después de todo lo que te hemos dado," "Eres peor que el 'drogadicto' de tu hermano." "Preferiría que hubieras quedado embarazada." "No eres nada más que una decepción para tu padre y para mí." "Espero que Dios te castigue para le tengas que rogar de rodillas que salve hija."* I begged my mother not to tell my father, I remember crying uncontrollably on my knees pleading her not to but she told him that same night. I didn't hear my father speak to me or refer to me for the next two months.

Here, the student marks the moment or moments which turned their world upside down. This rupture was both an ending and a beginning, an end to the life lived previously and the first step in a new beginning.

Nepantla

On the path of conocimiento, the provocation of el arrebato propels you into the second stage of nepantla. Nepantla is a "liminal or transitional space" (Anzaldúa, 2002, p. 544) where you might confront the conflicting realities of your existence. In nepantla, the old and the new, the ideal and the reality, even the desired and the undesired come face to face. Anzaldúa describes it as "the zone between changes when you struggle to find equilibrium between the outer expression of change and your inner relationships to it" (2002, pp. 548-49). It is here, despite the pain that these confrontations may cause, that you might glimpse the possibilities for transformation. Facing your various hybridities and valuing your contradictions for the insight they give, instills a promise of possibility and change.

One young woman wrote eloquently about being the child of immigrants and being continually locked into a conflict between the place her parents came from and the country she called home. Describing this moment in nepantla, she writes:

> My parents spoke English at work, but they also spoke Telugu. This didn't translate very well for me growing up. I was enrolled in daycare when I was about 18 months old. This meant that I started speaking English more than Telugu… In every family

video you watch of me above the age of two, you'll find that I'm speaking English. If my mother speaks to me in Telugu, I'll respond in English. I can't help it: my parents may be Indian-American, but it feels like I don't have much of a claim to either. I'm not nothing: I have an identity that has been influenced by the cultures I grew up in. Some days, it's fluid and changes between my parents' version of Indian culture and the American values I got from school. Other times, there's this total disconnect. Maybe sometimes it's a perfect blend.

Another student described the experience of being stuck in a liminal space between two ethnicities unable to satisfactorily fulfill the tacit expectations of either side of the duality: "I didn't realize I was considered 'different' until I was in 4th grade when another Hispanic student asked, 'how are you Mexican and don't speak Spanish?' From then on, I grew up hearing, 'you're too white for the Mexicans and too Mexican for the whites.'" In both of these cases, the students experience nepantla as a space of conflict, a space where opposing perspectives clash. But nepantla is also a space from which you become inspired to grow and change, where the conflict gives you the ability to see new opportunities for growth.

The Coatlicue State

But for you to grow, desconocimientos, or ignorances, must be faced. This, in turn, can throw you into the Coatlicue state, the third stage, where "you cling to your misery" (Anzaldúa, 2002, p. 550) and embrace the comfort of your ignorances. Here, you "retreat into fantasies," "succumb to your addiction of choice," and wallow in your own victimhood (Anzaldúa, 2002, p. 552). Wounds surface but you are not ready to dive in and listen to the lessons the wounds are capable of sharing. One student recounted the difficulty of dealing with sexual assault and trying to move past it and love oneself again:

> What an incredible feat it is to be a woman. To be raised afraid, and to be aged afraid. I sometimes wake up seeing my body as my own; there is no more disgust or anger. Why should I look at my body in these ways when I was not the one who hurt it? In these moments, I often realize the pain has just moved to a different part of me, and it will likely come back again. Afterall, feeling obligated to love myself is different than truly loving myself.

Her piece reads with palpable emotion and connects her own experience with that of many other women. Similarly, another student wrote about the reality women face of shared desconocimientos.

But it is not just our individual desconocimientos that plague us. We are also held back from growth and transformation by the willful ignorances maintained by the societies and cultures we reside in. One young woman wrote honestly and sincerely about the desconocimientos impacting her generation:

> I was 16 when Donald Trump got elected. I was 18 when a genocide in the country I'm from becomes the biggest humanitarian crisis of the 21st century. I'm 19 and

there is a global, tragic pandemic. Just as I turn 20, a monumental civil rights movement erupts, advocating for racial justice and equality. I'm 21 and am witnessing the effects of the unavoidable, catastrophic climate crisis unfold... there was never a conscious moment when I wasn't watching social politics affect my life every day. It's hard to be a passionate young woman and not be angry all the time.

Movement out of the Coatlicue State and transformation comes when you have faced and taken ownership of your desconocimientos. When you finally acknowledge the destructive nature of your wounds, healing will begin. Processing the pain and self-destruction incites change. For this last student, the wounds of her generation are not enough to hold her in place. Though it is hard to be angry constantly and "[l]iving a feminist life is emotional labor and it is truly exhausting," she writes that, "When you come of age in such a profound time, you make a choice... I made my choice- I decided to fight."

The Call

The fourth stage, or "the call," prompts you to alter your thoughts and behavior; to (re)shape and (re)member your narratives. It is a call to leave behind what does not work and enact change. Anger and self-doubt become constructive. This process of personal archaeology is painful but not as painful as living with one's desconocimientos (Anzaldúa, 2002, p. 557). You "compose yourself anew and differently" (Anzaldúa, 2002, p. 558). Throughout "the call," your perceptions shift. You recognize the radical interconnectivity that connects you via spirit to all that exists "you are becoming, not who you have been" (Anzaldúa, 2015, p. 135). For one student, that acknowledgement came when, late one night, she recognized the shared danger of being a woman:

> It was three o'clock in the morning, I was a couple streets down from the nightlife area, and not in the best part of town when I saw her. A woman appearing to be in her early twenties alone, stumbling in heels... I heard the voice—*you've been there, too...* It was a chance to practice a part of feminism that I had been learning about: to protect. As I turned around, pulled over and rolled my window down, she was visibly intoxicated and had appeared to be crying. I offered her a ride and when she hesitated, I turned on the lights, put my hands up, and said, "I know what it's like and I understand—I'm a woman, too—but I'm not going to hurt you. This is just not the safest place to be walking alone." She got into the back seat and as I drove her a few more streets over... two strangers bonded over an unspoken understanding.

In "the call," Anzaldúa highlights how your identities are relational and interconnected. Anzaldúa writes that here "[i]t dawns on you that *you're not contained by your skin-* you exist outside your body... If the body is energy, is spirit—it doesn't have boundaries" (2015, p. 134). Given this realization, perception shifts. The silos that keep you separated from other individuals start to come down and the role of community becomes important. The desire to (re)define yourself relationally propels you to disentangle your many identities from their narratives and consider how the pieces might fit back together in a new narrative that better suits who you are becoming.

Putting Coyolxauhqui Together

Next, in "putting Coyolxauhqui together," the fifth stage, you shed old versions of your bodymindspirit and piece together new narratives of bodymindspirit that support a connectionist mode of existing in the world and a "more expansive conocimiento" (Anzaldúa, 2002, p. 560) that nurtures you to see the commonalities that bind all living beings, rather than the differences that divide. Having listened to the lessons of your past wounds, this stage is where you create new meanings of the self and compose new narratives of understanding because it is not enough to overcome your desconocimientos, you must construct a vision of an alternative bodymindspirit to propel you forward. For the transgender student, "putting Coyolxauhqui together" meant acknowledging their new gender as a man:

> I couldn't deny that fact anymore. I had to own up to myself and accept the truth of who I really was… I felt so free being able to finally be me and not have this thing in the back of my head controlling me and holding me back anymore. I was finally me… Finally, being in love with myself gave me the confidence to help and support others who could be going through the same struggles that I did my whole life and hopefully help them to find love for themselves just as I did.

This student (re)constructs a new narrative of self that is more in line with the bodymindspirit they seek to become. One which better enables them to enact growth and change.

A Clash of Realities

But those "insidious desconocimientos" (Anzaldúa, 2002, p. 564) bring about a sixth stage, a "clash of realities," where you confront again your own denials and those denials of society. You bring your new bodymindspirit into the proverbial sunlight only to find the new narrative you have created is not as expansive or affirmative as you proposed. For the transgender student, living as a man brought them face to face with a new way of noticing various inequalities that they had to come to terms with:

> Since coming out as trans, I am treated like a man in every space I am in. I quickly noticed how much better I was being treated by other people. I had so much unearned respect from other women and especially men. When I identified as a woman no one ever went out of their way for me. People constantly interrupted me, cut me off on the sidewalk, I was always being mansplained and so much more. Now those things don't happen to me anymore just because the world sees me as a man.

Here, the student is called upon to deepen their awareness and make sense of their new narrative in a broader sense that includes not only their life story, but the life stories of others as well.

Spiritual Activism

Throughout this process of gaining conocimiento, realities shift, and you enact a seventh process, spiritual activism. Spiritual activism is where the insights gained by your bodymindspirit on the path of conocimiento, become directed outward as actions aimed at creating social justice. You have gained consciousness, and that consciousness is a conversation that exists between you and your community. Spiritual activism is spirituality[1] intentionally directed at creating social change. It is the place where us and them no longer exist in silos. As Anzaldúa puts it, "We live in each other's pockets, occupy each other's territories, live in close proximity and intimacy with each other" (2000, p. 254). With an intentional focus on social justice, the students shared their autohistoria-teorías in a virtual colloquium. Their sharing of their narratives connected in this venue provided them with a complex and hybrid form of subjectivity. Each student acknowledged that as they presented their narrative, their truth, they also told a shared truth, one interwoven with profound challenges to the presumed boundaries between I and you. And so, when one student defiantly read, "I am woman, I am lesbian, I am feminist, I am Hispanic, I am first gen, I am agnostic, I am a sexual assault survivor, I am strong, I am powerful. I am," she not only healed herself, she created the opportunity for others like her to do the same.

CONCLUSION

After completing their autohistoria-teorías, I challenged the students to think of their narratives as feminist theory. I called upon the example of Cherríe Moraga's "theory in the flesh" from *This Bridge Called My Back* where she writes, "A theory in the flesh means one where the physical realities of our lives- our skin color, the land or concrete we grew up on, our sexual longings- all fuse to create a politic born of necessity" (Anzaldúa & Moraga, 2015, p. 19) and asked my students to consider how their pieces could be used in a classroom or in the larger feminist movement to elucidate various struggles for equality, organize around social justice concerns, and ultimately decolonize/ up-end/ dismantle our very ideas about what theory should be about and sound like. Given my students' reservations about the theories they had engaged with previously and how those theories had not represented their lived realities, I expected them to see this value in their own narratives. Surprisingly, out of all the many ways I worked to push my students outside of their comfort zones in the writing of their narratives, this

---

[1] Spirituality here is the sense of radical interconnectivity that allows us to believe in the existence of something sacred and transcendent through which we postulate a shared onto-epistemology.

was the hardest leap for them to take. Having been indoctrinated thoroughly in the academy, each student hesitated in valuing their own personal story in the same way they had been led to value the theories of others. It took concerted effort and a thorough deconstruction of the value and purpose of feminist theory itself before most, (sadly, I never convinced all of them,) that theory was of value when it connected personal experience to social realities and hadn't their narratives of lived experience done exactly that?

Moreover, I prodded them to consider how their theories of inequalities, pains, cultural critique, self-growth, and healing might ultimately transform how we envision and use theory in the academy. Epistemologically, autohistoria-teoría recognizes the importance of lived experience as a vital knowledge making endeavor. Ontologically, the writing of these narratives acknowledges that we can create and recreate our realities in the same way we tell our fictions. This ability was extremely important to Anzaldúa's process of discovery and knowledge-making. In *Borderlands/La Frontera*, she writes, that "I write the myths in me, the myths I am, the myths I want to become" (2007, p. 93). Rather than always forcing students to make sense of theoretical musings and experiences which they as BIPOC and queer students might have no relation to, the crafting of autohistoria-teorías creates opportunities to understand why it is we theorize to begin with, while locating their experiences within realm of communal understanding. The crafting and creation of autohistoria-teoría within the academy upends our very assumptions about knowledge-making while simultaneously exposing the limitations of those existing paradigms and canonical methods of theorizing. Moreover, the narratives exist as crucial forms of sociopolitical resistance that work to dismantle the master's house from within.

ACKNOWLEDGEMENT

Special thanks to all the students in the capstone course for their hard work and inspiration.

REFERENCES

Anzaldúa, G. E. (2002). "now let us shift… the path of conocimiento… inner work, public acts." *This Bridge We Call Home* (pp. 540–78) (G. E. Anzaldúa & A. L. Keating, Eds.). Routledge..

Anzaldúa, G. E. (2007). *Borderlands/La Frontera* (4th ed.). Aunt Lute Books.

Anzaldúa, G. E. (2000). Toward a Mestiza Rhetoric: Gloria Anzaldúa on Composition, Postcoloniality, and the Spiritual. Interview with Andrea Lunsford. *Interviews/Entrevistas* (pp. 251–80) (A. L. Keating, Ed.). Routledge.

Anzaldúa, G. E. (2015). *Light in the dark/ Luz en los oscuro* (A. L. Keating, Ed.). Duke UP.

Anzaldúa, G. E., & Moraga, C. (2015). Entering the lives of others: Theory in the flesh. *This bridge called my back.* (4th ed., G. Anzaldúa & C. Moraga, Eds., p. 19). State University of New York Press.

PART II

LIVED EXPERIENCES/IDENTITIES

CHAPTER 7

BLACK ART VISUALITY

(Re)Directing the Black Gaze in Art Education

Indira Bailey
Artist

The significance of seeing positive images of yourself is vital to understanding your identity and culture. Art shows the viewer how to visualize the past, present, and future. Often the pictures of Black culture distort or misconstrue reality. This chapter explains the significance of seeing and looking at Black artwork from a different gaze and spectatorship than the traditional western canon. The author, a Black artist and art educator, describes the influence and exposure of Black art visuality that (re)shifts the gaze, (re)directs spectatorship, and (re)sees social differences of the Black community. The author describes how they (re)create the Black gaze through three paintings in this chapter. Through a critical visual methodology of how images are produced, circulated, represented, and experienced, the author suggests ways for teachers, curriculum developers, and administration to incorporate Black art visuality into the classroom to develop a deeper appreciation for Black artists' contributions to art education.

I remember watching the 1970s T.V. sitcom *Good Times* based in Chicago's public housing projects as a little girl. This T.V. show represented the Black nuclear family in a loving, two-parent, working-class household focused on racial injustice, socio-economic challenges, and community relations (Coleman & Lawrence, 2019). One of the main characters is an artist named J.J. Evans Jr. Most of the paintings featured on the T.V. show by the character J.J. are painted by artist Ernie Barnes. In many of the episodes, Barnes' painting, the *Sugar Shack*, was one of the show's main images during their opening and closing credits. The *Sugar Shack* is full of emotions, with Black people dancing, socializing, and enjoying life. Barnes created this painting to recall his childhood experience of witnessing how Black people use the rhythmic movement of dance to release physical tension (Coleman & Lawrence, 2019). *Good Times* was my first exposure to visualizing Black culture through the art of a Black American community.

Black art has a magnetic force that pulls you to see the richness of history and culture. Television shows like *Good Times* brought Black art visuality into many households in Black communities and the American public creating critical spectatorship (hooks, 1992). Black artists' artistry is not new; however, many Black communities are unaware of their contributions. The *Sugar Shack* painting reinforced Black spectatorship to see the vitality of Black artwork and Black culture. Because of my early exposure to Black art, as a high school art educator, I felt responsible for displaying artists of color and my own artwork in the class that reflected the students' environment. Students of color rarely see artwork reflecting their history, culture, and communities. I was concerned that the Black and Brown students in the art class would not appreciate the artwork of artists from their culture because of the limited exposure to them. I painted in the classroom to show the students that Black people paint. I wanted them to see I was not just their art teacher; I was also a Black artist.

Black art visuality engages race, identity, history, and memories that offer a different gaze and spectatorship than the white western art canon. I aim to provide students the opportunity and understanding to create their realities based on their culture, which ultimately influences how they interpret images and visually look at the world. In this chapter, I use Black art visuality to reflect on my experiences as an art educator and artist. My aim is not to compare my artistic method to another artist or define Black art visuality in other modes of the arts. I will discuss how I produce a Black artist's gaze to promote Black spectatorship in three of my paintings. Finally, I suggest ways of incorporating Black art visuality into art education through a critical visual methodology.

(RE)SHIFTING VISUALITY

In the 1830s, Scottish transcendentalist Thomas Carlyle coined visuality as a state or quality of being visual or mental/spiritual visuality (Sand, 2012). Visuality association with visual perspectives and cultural structures began with the experience of seeing and representing images. Art historian Alexa Sand (2012) explains Carlyle's physiology and spiritual perception shifted to physical appearance and then to art historians investigating how people previously viewed objects studied today. Visual culturalist Gillian Rose (2016) expounds on the definition of visuality in various ways. Vision is constructed based on how people are able, allowed, and made to see an image. Other scholars considered visuality the positionality of being visual in a culture and not a specific art medium (Sturken & Cartwright, 2009). Visuality has transformed from mental vision, physicality, and cultural constructions throughout history. The investigation of how race and gender apply to these definitions is imperative. Sand (2012) further highlights, "Visuality asks us to look differently at familiar objects but also to turn our gaze on objects resistant to the traditional methods of our discipline" (p.91). Black artists provide an abundance of such objects through their artwork. The refusal to accept the western art canon constructions of Blackness visually presented as reality seeks a different definition of visuality.

Black Art Visuality

Black feminist theorist Tina Campt describes Black visuality as multiple frequencies of looking at Black culture through the practice of refusal (2018, 2019). She challenges the construction of the traditional western definition of visuality by questioning the depiction of Black people. In many Black communities, the opportunities to see art representing their environment and experiences are limited. Moreover, Campt (2021) claims a Black perspective does not constantly challenge the "existing framework for viewing Blackness" (p. 19). In other words, exhibiting and looking at Black art does not mean a cultural and historical understanding of the image. Black visual artists create new outlets that broaden what I call "Black art visibility" by producing artwork that invokes memories, reveals historical accounts, communicates lived experiences, and promotes the discussion of the Black gaze.

Black art visuality confronts the mainstream art world's constructed biases not always acknowledged in many art museums, educational institutions, and art resources. Incorporating art with Black visuality, the artist has the power to (re)direct the western gaze to ways of seeing the lives of Black people. The western gaze in the art world constructs what art teachers see, teach, and present to the students. Ultimately, the students learn about artists from their environment and culture based on whose gaze is creating the curriculum. Black art visuality challenges the need for dramatic changes in art education to incorporate the Black gaze and spectatorship to dispute the mainstream art world notion of promoting diversity by exhibiting a Black portrait.

(RE)DIRECTING SPECTATORSHIP

The spectator's gaze is the "relationship between the subject who looks and other people, institutions, places, and objects in the world" (Sturken & Cartwright, 2009, p. 102). The relationship between the person who sees and the practice of looking is essential in creating and interpreting images. The relationship of the spectator's gaze is critical in students' analysis of race, gender, and social status. The white spectatorship has provided an unrealistic gaze of the Black community, which many believed to be factual or humorous. Spectatorship based on power and domination, whether consciously or unconsciously, affects Black art's interpretation. Interestingly art historian Patrick Frank (2019) claims,

> Looking is habitual and implies taking in what is before us in a generally mechanical or goal-oriented way.... Seeing is more open, receptive, and focused version of looking. In seeing, we look with our memories, imagination, and feeling attached. We take in something with our eyes, and then we remember similar experiences, or we imagine other possible outcomes, or we allow ourselves to feel something about it. We are doing more than looking (p. 13).

Black art illustrates memories through visual narration that can focus Black spectatorship on seeing a different perspective. The Black community is seen through a racist gaze of rejection as the norm to confuse our understanding of looking versus seeing. Many Black artists' artwork (re)directs the gaze to show historical, cultural, and societal events that paid homage to their rich legacy. They deconstruct the white gaze to teach a memorable moment. For example, Ernie Barnes' *Sugar Shack* was not the first Black artist to consciously paint Black life; however, his painting profoundly represented Black culture during the 1970s. Even in the 1920s, artist Archibald Motley painted the Black life of the Harlem Renaissance that contradicted racist stereotyped images of the Black community (re)directing Black spectatorship into a conscious act.

(Re)directing the gaze to students involves more than showing Black artwork during Black History Month or pretty paintings of Black people. An open conversation about race, culture, and identity is needed to introduce the social practice of looking. Students of color are seeking images they can relate to and discuss. I gathered Black art from magazines, greeting cards, calendars, and exhibition brochures when my students of color sought artists that looked like them for inspiration. Art educators can dismantle the power structure by seeking Black artists beyond western teaching resources. Scholars Marjorie and Brent Wilson (2009) explain how art affects children's perceptions, "Art holds up the images of culture as a mirror in which we can see ourselves reflected" (p. 66). I observed the difference in how students responded to art when I showed them an artist of color. (Re)directing the gaze from western-based textbooks to looking at images created by artists of color provides a sense of pride in representing your culture.

Children are natural and curious spectators and exposing their art to what mirrors their culture can influence how they see the world, see themselves, and develop their artistic skills (Wilson & Wilson, 2009). The artwork on *Good Times* exposed and influenced how I painted, but mostly, how I identified with Black culture early. As I reflect on my childhood, I am disappointed that I did not learn or see Black artwork in school. bell hooks spoke about the power of looking and fascination for children's gaze (1992). Teaching children the power of the gaze and spectatorship introduces them to histories, experiences, and cultures often obscured in curricula.

(RE)SEEING SOCIAL DIFFERENCES

Art education must first acknowledge Black artists' existence to incorporate Black art visuality. Discussing social differences dismantles the construction and stereotypes that Black people are not talented artists. Rose (2016) states five aspects of critically examining the effect and structure of visual images: (a) visualizing social differences, (b) looking at images, (c) differentiating visual culture, (d) circulation of images, and (e) the agency of images. These five aspects of critically examining visual images create social categories many used to marginalize Black artists and underrepresent them in K-12 art education teaching resources. For example, the textbook *The Visual Experience* 3rd Edition by Davis Publications for high school art students displays approximately three Black women and eight Black male artists out of a 500-page book. Even though this book highlights art history, art media, art lessons, and the principles and elements of design, there are limited artists of color for students to learn. Many racialized art education textbooks cater primarily to publishing white artists exhibited in the white museums.

Art education is rooted in whiteness that normalizes racism in teaching practice and curriculum development (Dewhurst, 2019; Wolfgang, 2019). Art educators must develop a consciousness of (re)seeing and visualizing the social differences in their textbooks, posters, and videos to aid art instruction. Black art visuality challenges the social and cultural construction of images through Blackness. While textbooks such as *The Visual Experience* is a source to circulate pictures to teach students the fundamentals of art, they can also be harmful to students of color who want to learn about the lived experiences of Black artists. To understand Black art visuality is to acknowledge a different gaze that includes racial oppression, suppressed history, and cultural identities of Black people. Many Black artists construct their agency through Black art visuality opening the critical discussion of power, race, and gender. These displays of Black life are rarely taught in school or exhibited in museums and galleries.

(RE)CREATING A BLACK GAZE

In following Campt's (2021) definition of the Black gaze as "a structure of visual engagement that implicitly and explicitly understands blackness as neither singular nor a singularity; it embraces instead the multiplicity of blackness" (p.43), I aim to be an example as a Black artist and (re)shift the Black culture's gaze. Through my creative process that portrays Black lives to produce a Black gaze to transform the viewer's standpoint, I teach and show Black art. In teaching the spectrum of Blackness that includes the transnational gaze, students learn about the African diaspora cultures, customs, languages, socioeconomics, and religions. While I do not attempt to analyze another Black artist's style and purpose, I understand not every Black artist paint Blackness. However, I follow Frank's comment as "the artist is the source or sender of any work put on view; the work itself is the means of carrying the message (p. 16)." I deliberately (re)create a message about

Black people that introduces and communicates their stories to an audience that may or may not be familiar with their lives.

The importance of Black art visuality is in how an image looks and is seen by spectators who have their agenda and social constructions (Rose, 2016; Sturken & Cartwright, 2009). While I cannot control how a person may look at my artwork, I can control what I paint and attempt to (re)direct the gaze and engage in spectatorship that challenges the white norm of looking at Black people and Black art.

THE ARTIST'S GAZE

Art is a form of visual literacy that aids in uncomfortable conversations. This section features three paintings I created and explained my gaze to highlight the Black experience locally and globally.

The first painting, *Sunday Morning* (Figure 7.1), highlights Black culture and shows the experience of many Black little girls having their hair hot combed or straightened.[1] In this painting, the mother is straightening her daughter's hair. The little girl closes her eyes and squinches her face waiting for this process to be over. The mother carefully holds the daughter's hair to straighten and not burn her. I remember bending my head down so my mother could straighten the "kitchen."[2] I also remember the smell of heated hair and feeling my mother's breath blowing on the hot comb to cool it down. My mother would yell, "Hold your head still." For many Black women, having their hair hot combed was a ritual on Saturday night or Sunday morning before church.

When most non-Black people look at this image, they see a mother combing her daughter's hair. They do not see the cultural implications clear to most Black women. This painting reminds Black people of their mother or grandmother in her nightgown, turning the stove on, and placing the wooden handle and metal comb on the stove burner. Black women who had their hair straightened remember the pressing oil on the back of their mother's hand to smooth the edges. When your mother finished pressing your hair, you could not run around for fear of sweating your hair out. This painting is not just about a mother combing her daughter's hair; it is a memory and a feeling about Black identity, community, womanhood, and assimilation that is missed in the discussion of art if you cannot identify with the culture.

The second oil painting is called *Zaynah* (Figure 7.2). *Zaynah* (fictitious name) is a Black Moroccan. I met her during my six-week Fulbright scholarship to Morocco in the restaurant of a remote rural village on the outskirts of the Sahara Desert. She was one of the workers in the restaurant. After I ate, I walked to the back of the restaurant to see the garden, and she was standing there. When I painted her,

---

[1] Black women primarily use hot combing to straighten their curly or coarse textured hair. A hot comb is heated up to 500 degrees to straighten hair. https://nmaahc.si.edu/explore/stories/sizzle

[2] The "kitchen" refers to the hair at the nape of the neck. This area of hair was the most resistant or the kinkiest to straighten. https://www.naturallycurly.com/curlreading/kinky-hair-type-4a/naturally-speaking-more-about-the-kitchen

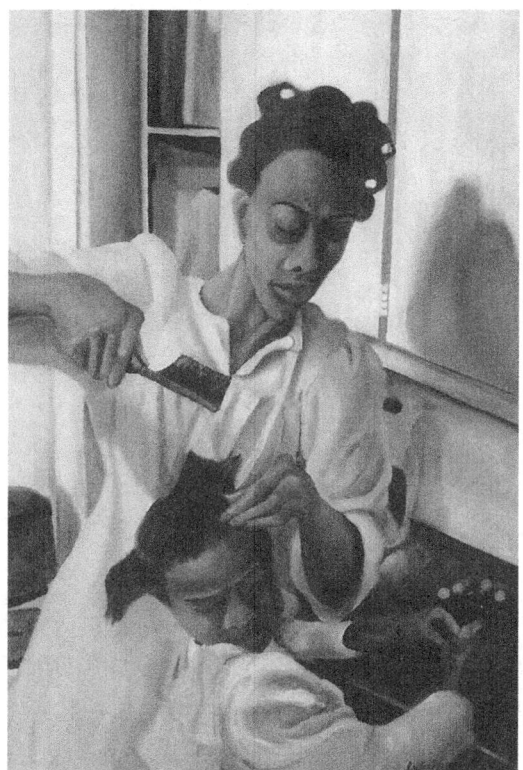

FIGURE 7.1. Indira Bailey, Sunday Morning, 1990, Oil on Canvas, 24X28 (Courtesy of the artist)

I wanted the audience to see more than a portrait of an African Muslim woman wearing a hijab in Morocco. *Zaynah* is unseen. She is an essential worker. Most people traveling do not stop and take the time to see her reality. The traditional western gaze stereotypes *Zaynah*'s race, gender, and religious belief.

Zaynah challenges the audience's gaze in how they look at her and whether they reject, sympathize, or advocate for her. I painted *Zaynah* to create Black spectatorship that questioned African Muslim women's social and religious constructions. Some people will look at her and see limited opportunities in education, financial freedom, social status, and gender equality. Other people see a provider, strength, power, and devotion. In (re)directing the gaze to include race, gender, and religion, the spectator challenges their ideologies of spirituality.

My third painting, a watercolor painting, is titled *Coconut Man* (Figure 7.3). I met this Afro Panamanian man in Portobelo, Panama, an UNESCO World Heritage Site, during a three-week artist residency. In the mornings, I would speak to him at his coconut stand. What intrigued me about him is that he is also unseen.

FIGURE 7.2. Indira Bailey, Zaynah, 28X30, Oil on Canvas, (Courtesy of the artist)

The tourists looked at an exotic person delightfully opening green coconuts to drink the juice with a colorful straw and return to their cruise ships. I saw a hidden gem from a Black gaze, a Congo descendant living in a rural village surrounded by tropical forests.

The *Coconut Man* tells what people do not see beyond the tourist sites. The hot, steamy days watching strangers walk by, hoping they purchase a coconut to earn a daily wage. I intentionally painted the *Coconut Man* to (re)shift the gaze that reflects Black culture globally for an audience to do more than look at a watercolor painting of a man selling coconuts. Afro Panamanians experience similar racism as African Americans based on their skin color, which is rarely depicted in art. Having Afro Latinx students in my class, I understand the significance of painting this series to see their heritage. I also understood the importance of Black

FIGURE 7.3. Indira Bailey, Coconut Man, 28X24, Watercolor (Courtesy of the artist)

American students seeing the commonalities of their culture, race, and history merged with the Afro Latinx communities.

These three paintings are only a few that show the rich history and diversity of Black people. Through these paintings, I construct the Black gaze to reject the western canon standards of beauty and artistic talent. Regardless of whether the subject is regional or global, I call attention to their Blackness. I will not say my paintings are only for a Black audience; however, I consider the cultural text to invoke a response to seeing the plight in Black life. My goal is for Black people and students to resonate with the image and see someone who identifies with their culture, environment, and experience.

INCORPORATING BLACK VISUALITY INTO ART EDUCATION

I include Rose's critical visual methodology to analyze Black art visuality in art education. Rose (2016) proposes various approaches to looking at images through four sites: production, audience, image, and circulation. While Rose's critiques on visualizing images lay the foundation for visual culture critics, I adopt her method of visualizing social effects to create Black art visual materials for the K-12 art education. A critical Black art investigation can significantly aid art teachers in structuring how images are produced, represented, circulated, and experienced by the student.

Restructuring critical visual methodology into practical art education methods engages art teachers to think critically and consciously about Black art visuality. The goal of (re)directing the gaze is to practice looking beyond historical and racial stereotypes. Introducing students to Black artists can help them identify with their culture and create artwork through a Black gaze. Showing Black art to non-Black students is vital to developing a deeper appreciation of Black artists' contributions to the art field. I developed suggestions to incorporate Black art visuality into your teaching practice.

The Creation of Black Art

Black artists create art in various mediums and styles. Consider functional or practical art, for example, the sweetgrass basket by Mary Jackson. Also, consider Black graphic designers and animators.

- What other non-tradition forms of artwork do Black artists use?
- How do Black artists create artwork that shows their heritage?

Locating Black Artists

Black artists are everywhere—contact or visit local community galleries, museums, and social media sites. Most local artists are more than willing to come and talk to students. Ask students if they know or are related to any Black artists.

- Are there Black artists in the community, local galleries, or art organizations?
- What non-art resources can I gather of Black art?

Understanding How Black Images are Circulated

The importance for art teachers is to look beyond the typical art education catalog to locate Black art. Understand that Black art may not be highly visible; therefore, patience is required.

- Buy books of or by Black artists.
- Collect calendars, greeting cards, stamps, and magazine covers. For example, illustrator Alexander Bostic created the 2022 Edmonia Lewis stamp.

Know Your Students

Creating a curriculum is not just writing a lesson plan; it requires the teacher to consider their audience. Your students are your audience. Students of color desire to see artwork by artists that look like them. As they learn about white artists, it is essential to know about Black and other artists of color. The same is true for non-Black students; learning about Black artists is valuable. Seeing artwork that reflects their culture could motivate them and increase their creativity.

- Does the image reflect the student's history and heritage?
- How do I make sure students of color are included in the artmaking process to express their culture?

These are only a few suggestions to bring Black art visuality into the curriculum and classroom. The goal is not to create a list of Black artists and save them for Black History Month. The aim is to introduce students to Black artists and their images to incorporate a different form of visuality into your teaching practice.

CONCLUDING THOUGHTS

There is a difference between looking at and seeing images in Black artwork. Artwork can (re)direct the gaze toward Black spectatorship in seeing the Black perspective of struggle, pain, oppression, love, faith, family, and community. The western gaze is prevalent in educational institutions, museums, pre-service programs, teaching resources, and art education at large.

In a traditional art education program, we look at the artwork, the styles, and the artist's techniques. Nevertheless, when we consciously see that Black art creates the stories of lived experience, we become more receptive and open to the message. Through this process, as art educators, we can assist students in allowing themselves to feel, remember, and imagine a world familiar with their culture, heritage, and history. By viewing artwork by artists of color, art educators can help students "understand what happens in the process of looking by taking into account both the conscious and unlevel levels of viewer experience" (Sturken & Cartwright, 2009, p. 102).

Scholars define visuality in many ways; however, the main point is seeing how images influence and affect the spectator's behavior. Campt highlights how Black artists demonstrate Blackness through the Black gaze to challenge the western canon of art. Rose describes the critical visual methodology to access the creating and viewing of images. Black art visuality acknowledges Black spectatorship to critically look at the experience, history, and culture expressed through a Black artist's gaze. The whiteness in art education has demonstrated that they will ignore what they do not want to acknowledge. Selecting Black art to (re)direct the gaze allows students to see their story, culture, and history that delves into a deeper conversation than aesthetics to understand cultural attributes and experiences.

REFERENCES

Campt, T. (2018) *Black visual frequency: A glossary, Black Visuality.* Fotomuseum Winterthur https://www.fotomuseum.ch/en/series/black-visual-frequency-a-glossary/, August 8, 2018.

Campt, T. (2019). Black visuality and the practice of refusal. *Women & Performance: A Journal of Feminist Theory, 29*(1), 79–87.

Campt, T. (2021). *A Black gaze: Artists changing how we see.* The MIT Press.

Coleman, R., & Lawrence, N. (2019). Fix it Black Jesus: The Iconography of Christ in Good Times. *Religions, 10*(7), 410.

Dewhurst, M. (2019). Reflecting on a paradigm of solidarity? Moving from niceness to dismantle whiteness in art education. [Whiteness and Art Education]. *Journal of Cultural Research in Art Education 36*(1), 147–165.

Frank, P. (2019). *Prebles' artforms* (12th ed.). Pearson.

hooks, b. (1992). *Black looks: Race and representation.* South End Press.

Rose, G. (2016). *Visual methodologies: An introduction to researching with visual materials* (4th ed.).Sage Publications.

Sand, A. (2012). Visuality. [Medieval art history today—Critical terms]. *Studies in Iconography, 33,* 89–95.

Sturken, M., & Cartwright, L. (2009). *Practices of looking: An introduction to visual culture.* Oxford University Press.

Wilson, M., & Wilson, B. (2009). *Teaching children to draw* (2nd ed.). Davis Publications.

Wolfgang, C. (2019). The white supremacy of art education in the United States: My complicity and path toward reparation pedagogy. [Whiteness and Art Education]. *Journal of Cultural Research in Art Education 36*(1), 14–28.

CHAPTER 8

PAPER THIN BOUNDARIES

Glynnis Reed
The Pennsylvania State University

In my photographic series, *Paper Thin Boundaries*, I explore identity and place within the context of one's relationship with the self in the physical, social, and psychological geographies of the city and nature. The work features representations of urban graffiti and the Black female body, specifically self-portrait images, set in a sublime landscape. The title of the body of work refers to personal boundaries—the psychological space that we use to separate ourselves from one another. Here, boundaries also refer to borders, and the way we may perceive someone from another country or culture. I began this work while on an artist residency in Austria, years prior to the COVID-19 pandemic. During this residency, I lived in a small town in Lower Austria for two and a half months where there were very few people of color. As an African American woman artist, my difference was quite pronounced in that environment. This series of artworks reflects my gradual response to looking out at the other and being seen as other in Europe in the early 2010s.

In this series, I use graffiti to represent a forum for the expression of divergent voices, calling out seemingly anonymously, sometimes as cries for help and sometimes as powerful assertions of self, identity, and protest. This idea connects to the fact that I am using my own body in the work, and as an artist, I identify with this need to give voice to one's view of the world through visual imagery.

All of the source material for these digital collages are the many sites of graffiti-tagging, sgraffito, handwriting on walls, murals, and natural landscapes I photographed in Austria and Paris during my residency. The figure in this work is set against graffiti weaving and winding through space, hovering around and over the body. This graffiti is language made material, floating in space. I imagine graffiti's gestural marks as visualizations of the idiosyncratic sounds of human voices. The graffiti that I encountered in my travels during my residency was often rendered in German, so there was an inscrutability of the language for me as an outsider to the Austrian culture. Language differences were a barrier just as much as differences in race could be. I look at variances in race, gender, class, and nationality through this work questioning what it means to be, alternately, in the subject or object position.

Placing myself in front of the camera in my studio in Krems, Austria brought more performativity to my process of digital photography. This offered me more control of the image and my body within the frame. The figure in nature is a theme I have examined in my art for a number of years, and the female body in a sublime natural setting is a powerful subject for me. I find ideas about women's identities and the power, cycles, and beauty of nature to be a source of rich content to mine for my artwork. I defiantly produce these images of myself as a Black woman in nature despite the racist/patriarchal constructs about Blackness and femininity being innately associated with nature. Conventionally, women have been placed in a subjugated position of inferiority as "nature," to the white male identified "culture." In this formulation, nature is framed as closely identified with flesh and the body, as a binary opposition to "superior" male culture and mind.

My bare feet in the photographs suggest an illusion of physical connection to the landscape. However, the images are highly constructed; I photographed myself in my studio, so I was never actually barefoot in the grass. This barefootedness conveys a feeling of being "natural," and I wear simple clothing that shows the contours of my body. This constructedness of the collage approach emphasizes the sense of displacement of the Black female body in these settings, being out of place and artificially inserted into "foreign" locations.

These digital collages feature disparate elements brought together to form artificial moments in my life; I don't intend for these landscape compositions to be naturalistic, although they are photo-realistic and photo-based. To revisit the idea of boundaries, and the spaces between edges and shapes, I emphasize the sharpness of the edges of the figure against landscapes that I walked or hiked through in Austria. The blurred multiple exposure images of dirt, grass, trees, and layered graffiti seem suspended in space and time. These photographs express the contours and entanglements of my life as a marginalized subject in globalized temporal realities.

Paper Thin Boundaries • 73

FIGURE 8.1. Glynnis Reed, *A Season For All Things*, 2011. Archival inkjet print (Courtesy of the artist)

FIGURE 8.2. Glynnis Reed, *No One Else*, 2011. Archival inkjet print (Courtesy of the artist)

FIGURE 8.3. Glynnis Reed, *Fascination*, 2011. Archival inkjet print (Courtesy of the artist)

FIGURE 8.4. Glynnis Reed, *Obliteration*, 2011. Archival inkjet print (Courtesy of the artist)

Paper Thin Boundaries • 75

FIGURE 8.5. Glynnis Reed, *Down By the Water*, 2011. Archival inkjet print (Courtesy of the artist)

FIGURE 8.6. Glynnis Reed, *Cascade of Their Truth*, 2011. Archival inkjet print (Courtesy of the artist)

FIGURE 8.7. Glynnis Reed, *Patience*, 2011. Archival inkjet print (Courtesy of the artist)

FIGURE 8.8. Glynnis Reed, *Objection to Abjection*, 2011. Archival inkjet print (Courtesy of the artist)

CHAPTER 9

WHEN AND WHERE I ENTER

A Reflective Essay on the Photographic History of Three Generations of Black Women Educators

Meghan Green
Uplift Ascend Primary

Growing up in the prairies of south Louisiana, one learns the delicate balance between speaking the language of your home, the language of your peers, and the language of the establishment. This essay witnessed the sense of collective responsibility inherent in the work of Black women educators through an arts-based exploration of the intersectional lives of three generations of educators. Utilizing endarkened feminist epistemology and poetic inquiry, I reflected on the intricacies of my family's diverse experiences as Black women educators. I analyzed family photographs and transcripts of our intergenerational gatherings to re(member) the ways that we have brought ourselves into classrooms as Black women for over 60 years. Through the lens of daughtering, my grandmother, mother, and I learned pedagogical lessons to navigate the hegemonic spaces of dominant curricular spaces.

Black women often exist in spaces that require skills only learned from being someone's daughter. Evans-Winters (2019) described daughtering as "a way of being and navigating the social world" (p. 137). While we learn how to diligently take care of others during this process of understanding the social milieu of dominant settings, our community rarely teaches us how to take care of ourselves. My grandmother, mother, and I have taught in American public k-12 schools collectively, for 60 years. We have used the lessons we learned as daughters of the Jim Crow South, the Civil Rights Movement, and the hip hop generation to reinvent our pedagogy and actively dismantle dominant curricular discourses (Beauboeuf-Lafontant, 2005).

In the following reflective essay, I chose to use poetry to tell stories about the intersections of marginalized identities and pedagogical development. Poetry has sustained Black women for generations. From Audre Lorde and Nikki Giovanni to Ntozake Shange and Margaret Walker, Black women have used poetry to express what it feels like to live out our endarkened existences while smiling, laughing, crying, and fighting. Cutts (2019) proclaimed that "...in a field where Black women were never meant to survive (or thrive)" Black women researchers' use of poetry as a research method "demonstrates why writing is a necessity" (p. 913). Poetic inquiry grants qualitative researchers the opportunity to re-story the descriptive details of everyday life and craft pieces that hold deeper meaning (Cutts, 2019). I sought to witness three generations of Black women educators' ways of being and knowing through the lens of Dillard's (2000) endarkened feminist epistemology and poetic inquiry. Endarkened feminist epistemology can be understood as a means of expressing "how reality is known when based in the historical roots of Black feminist thought" (see Dillard, 2000, p. 662). How have my foremothers and I used the lessons learned from the margins of our identities to shape our pedagogy and beliefs as educators? To explore this question, I analyzed curated photographs to re(member) how we have brought ourselves into classrooms as Black women for over 60 years.

DAUGHTER OF THE JIM CROW SOUTH

Philippians 4:13

My grandmother is a praying woman.
The kind of woman who will speak life into you before she even shakes your hand.
Her words resonate because her faith is a result of acts unseen but felt.
My grandmother is a praying woman, after all.
The kind of woman who has seen the promise of hope through the specter of despair.
Her acts of service motivate because her strength is a result of steadfastness learned in the dark.

Born in 1937 to sharecroppers in a small community called Plaisance, Louisiana, my grandmother, Wiona Yvonne White Thomas, is a daughter of the Jim Crow South. Her earliest educational memories included a combination of practical lessons on maintaining a farm and the history of the people who came before her. She spent her youth within the four walls of a school built by her father's blood, sweat, and tears and the elders of her small mostly Black community. Residents built Plaisance School in 1919 as a Rosenwald school site. After graduating

FIGURE 9.1. My Grandmother, Wiona Yvonne White Thomas, at Grambling State University

from Plaisance School, she attended Grambling State University and earned her bachelor's degree in education. She then spent some time working in California after graduating in 1962. She later returned to Plaisance School, where she made history as the first woman hired as a Physical Education teacher. The late 1960s brought in the first wave of school integration in Saint Landry parish. My grandmother's next teaching assignment was as a 4th grade social studies teacher in the all-white neighboring community of Grand Prairie in 1969. She recalled an encounter with a white colleague during her first year of teaching in an integrated school. The colleague believed that my grandmother was changing history to suit her own needs. My grandmother reminded her that history is often taught based on understanding of the world.

The experiences of her family members had influenced my grandmother's understanding of the world as Black Creoles living in a society that saw them as a threat to the status quo. Her family owned the land they farmed. They intended to pass it down to their children and grandchildren. They had worked tirelessly to raise the necessary funds to build their own community school. My grandmother's pedagogy was rooted in her experiences of Ubuntu and "the length and breadth of Black history from the continent of Africa through its diaspora" (Dillard & Neal, 2020, p. 4). According to Dillard and Neal (2020), Ubuntu expresses the synergetic relationship between one's community and self. From the cadence of her mother's Creole dialect to the foods traditionally harvested and prepared, my grandmother's blackness informed her understanding of the world and impacted how she understood her role as an educator in the early years of integrated schools in south Louisiana.

My grandmother's commitment to preserving the history of her ancestors connected her to the idea of social activism for 33 years as an educator (Beauboeuf-Lafontant, 2005). As a history teacher in an environment with a contentious relationship with the community, she considered it her responsibility to pass the word on. She reflected on her experiences as one of the youngest daughters of fourteen children. Evans-Winters (2019) explained that "daughtering demands that you think for yourself and speak up for yourself and other people's daughters" (p. 138). My grandmother created a learning environment that promoted both individual and communal pride through intentional design. Students routinely engaged in research projects about people's lives across their farming community. These projects demonstrated how essential experiential knowledge of kinship ties, Indigenous healing practices, and collective narratives not highlighted in the state-sanctioned textbooks were.

DAUGHTER OF THE CIVIL RIGHTS MOVEMENT

Lady Writes the Blues

A poet speaks the truth around them.
> Her pen crafting lines that illuminate tight and cramped spaces meant to suppress.

A poet remembers things long forgotten.
> Her witty retorts reminding folks of exactly who she was.

A poet creates a relationship with empty spaces on the paper.
> Her words present shades of her favorite color as tranquil as a powder blue
> or as deep as a sapphire.

My mother, Priscilla Green, was born in Opelousas, Louisiana, on May 16, 1954, just one day before the U.S. Supreme Court decided Brown v. Board of Education. Perhaps this historic occasion signaled the path of resistance that she would one day forge. She spent kindergarten to 8th grade at North Elementary, the all-Black primary school in her northside community. In the 9th grade, she attended J.S. Clark High School, the all-Black secondary school in Opelousas. J.S. Clark was named after the first president of Southern University and A&M College in Baton Rouge. In 1969, Saint Landry parish allowed the first Black students to integrate Opelousas Senior High (OHS). My mother attended OHS from 10th through 12th grades. After graduating high school in the first integrated class, my mother went to Grambling State University to study Psychology and English Education.

FIGURE 9.2. My Mother, Priscilla A. Green, at Grambling State University

In 1979, she began teaching senior English Literature at Plaisance School. She brought the exuberance of youth and passion for Black literature inspired by her years at a historically Black college and university (HBCU). Education aims to empower and invite individuals to curate well-being spaces. Evans-Winters (2019) maintained that daughtering involves the intimate understanding that "the purpose of education was to help us bring forth…alternative and additional resources, skills, knowledge, and wisdom to our respective families and communities" (p 139). The creative spirit of educators also connects to the creativity daughters display in their roles. As daughters, we witness how our mothers move seamlessly between transdisciplinary worlds and offer insights into the world (Evans-Winters, 20219). These insights often take the form of prose and poetry and capture the complexities of what it means to exist within a racialized and sexualized multiverse.

My mother had always loved the written word. Her favorite genre was poetry, as she was an avid writer. She routinely shared her favorite literary pieces with her students. When discussing how she approached curriculum during her early years as an educator, she noted the importance of exposure. My mother channeled the passion contained in the literary works of Black authors across the diaspora. She combined these words with the knowledge of her community in an effort to "…center Black humanity, not just today but for centuries" within the curriculum (Dillard, 2022, p. 185). She passionately described how she filled her classrooms with books by Black authors. Blackness was centered in the learning spaces, not as an afterthought but by intentional design (Beauboeuf-Lafontant, 2005). My mother's penchant for Black literature extended into our home as well. The bookshelves in our living room included works from Maya Angelou, Toni Morrison, Alice Walker, and Margaret Walker. This early exposure to remarkable works of art by Black women greatly influenced my worldview and understanding of how stories were crafted (Cutts, 2019). I simultaneously saw myself reflected in the inquisitive femme presenting characters of Alice Walker and Zora Neale Hurston, while still feeling a sense of longing for words that described what it felt like to be both a womanist and an avid fan of a musical genre respite with misogynoir. This internal struggle represented the convergence of my understanding of one of the prevailing tenets of Black feminist thought: both/and. Black feminist theorists who employ an intersectional lens understand that the full extent of Black women's lived experiences can only be explained when considering how oppression operates simultaneously within the contexts of race, gender, and class.

DAUGHTER OF THE HIP HOP GENERATION

"Both/And Realities"

To exist somewhere between insider and outsider
Means that my experiences often simultaneously reflect a multitude of truths.
My intersections of identity create border spaces and messy explanations.
I accept these truths and serve them as offerings to those who attempt to define me.

FIGURE 9.3. My Graduation from Howard University

In 1984, I was born on Camp Pendleton, a Marines Corps Base Camp, in Oceanside, California on the cusp of two powerful sun signs: Libra and Scorpio. That alone gives me a combination of powers from both air and water elements. I embody a mixture of both intellect and passion; collaborative aims and individual desires; and silent perception and verbose expression. Evans-Winters (2019) expounded upon this conflict between self and communal responsibilities: "as daughters, we have come to believe that the purpose of knowledge pursuits is to identify and bring forth our individual (and collective) talents and abilities" (p. 140). As a Black daughter, I have worked hard to maintain an image of perfection while brilliantly failing to uphold the ideal of flawlessness. After graduating from high school, I decided to attend an HBCU like my grandmother and mother to identify my talents and abilities in an environment that had proven its effectiveness at nurturing the minds, souls, and hearts of Black women. I earned my undergraduate degree in Anthropology from Howard University in 2006 and then obtained my teaching certificate in 2007.

As an early childhood educator, I have often been the subject of various stereotypical perspectives. I do not fit neatly into boxes, and I embrace that. I have occupied the space of other my entire life. During adolescence, my sexual orientation placed me outside of the heteronormative milieu of my small town. I often struggled to identify my voice in the sea of rigid expectations in my Catholic household. I often questioned what my teachers taught me and longed to know more about the lived experiences of people who shared my intersections of identity. Combating the heteronormativity and misogynoir of Black spaces and the anti-blackness of LGBTQIA+ spaces, I was stuck in an infinite loop of explaining my ways of being and knowing to audiences who only acknowledged pieces of me. This identity crisis prompted my entrance into the discipline of early childhood education. My desire to end oppression through the vehicle of education is rooted in my early educational experiences as the exception to society's rules. I draw inspiration from my foremothers' experiences that provide the necessity for liberation through education. My teaching philosophy encourages me to examine the world and transform the societal ills critically. When asked why I became a teacher, I often reflect on the stories my grandmother and mother told me growing up near the soybean and sugar cane fields of southwest Louisiana. Stories about generations of students who passed through their classrooms, about families, and the importance of remembering who you are. These stories were always premised with the idea that knowing who you are was inherently tied to knowing where you were going.

The teaching practices of Black women educators embodies the spirit of Ubuntu (Dillard & Neal, 2020). My grandmother, mother, and I represent daughters from the Jim Crow south, the Civil Rights Movement, and the hip-hop generation. Our understandings of our roles as educators and daughters of the African Diaspora have inspired us to develop pedagogical stances that stand "unequivocally in opposition to colonial, neocolonial, and White supremacist scientific pursuits and propositions" (Evans-Winters, 2019, p. 140). As daughters of multiple generations, we understand the purpose of education: to represent our families and make our folks proud. To accomplish these goals, we must often interrupt hegemonic curriculum practices and construct the world we desire to thrive in based on our freedom dreams for future generations of daughters.

REFERENCES

Beauboeuf-Lafontant, T. (2005). Womanist lessons for reinventing teaching. *Journal of Teacher Education 56*(5), 436–445. https://doi.org/10.1177/0022487105282576

Cutts, Q. (2019). More than craft and criteria: The necessity of Ars spirituality in (Black women's) poetic inquiry and research poetry. *Qualitative Inquiry, 26*(7), 908–919. https://doi.org/10.1177/1077800419884966

Dillard, C. (2000). The substance of things hoped for, the evidence of things not seen: Examining an endarkened feminist epistemology in educational research and leadership. *International Journal of Qualitative Studies in Education, 13*(6), 661–681. https://doi.org/10.1080/09518390050211565

Dillard, C. (2022). *The spirit of our work: Black women teachers (re)member.* Beacon Press.

Dillard, C. B., & Neal, A. (2020). I am because we are: (Re)membering Ubuntu in the pedagogy of Black women teachers from Africa to America and back again. *Theory Into Practice, 59*(4), 370–378. https://doi.org/10.1080/00405841.2020.1773183

Evans-Winters, V. E. (2019). *Black feminism in qualitative inquiry.* Routledge.

CHAPTER 10

ode to cymone and will (ode is a really white, really funny word)

Samuel Jaye Tanner
The University of Iowa

strange moments in schools

1

this is an ode to cymone,
    ode is a funny word,
    a white word,
    makes me think of john keats,
it was 2004,
cymone was a poet,
    a 9th grader,
    a Black girl,
    a sister,
cymone's brother was will,
will was an actor,
    an 11th grader
    a Black boy,
    a brother,
i guess this is an ode to will, too—

or maybe it isn't,
maybe this is an ode to
    strange moments in schools,
teaching and learning
that makes space for something else,
    teachers giving up power,
    unscripted curriculums,
    making strange spaces,
spaces for students to speak against
    school,
    white supremacy,
or whatever—

white people often write about
    Black people,
white people often showcase their own celebrations of
    Black people,
(white people rarely disrupt white supremacy),
toni morrison wrote that
    the subject of the dream is the dreamer,
so even if i pretended to be writing about will and cymone here
    i'd mostly be writing about me,
i'm a white person who does
    strange things in schools,
this isn't an ode to me,
maybe it's an ode to memories of
    strange things in school,
and so maybe it's also an ode to will and cymone—

(or maybe this poem isn't an ode at all,
    i was never any good at defining literary terms—)

here's what i remember and i know and
    what i will tell in this poem:

2

cymone's was in my 9th grade english class,
will was in my 11th grade drama class,
it was 2004 and i was sam:
    a high school teacher
    a young white man,
    trying to love my students,
love is a funny word,
i don't mean it in a creepy way,
    or in a lame way,
i mean love in that strange
    lay down your life sort of way,
and i mean it when i say that i

tried to love my students,
i'm strange and i was strange,
strange because
    my parents were jewish immigrants,
    my parents were addicts,
    my childhood ended when i was seven,
i don't know,
but i do know i tried to love my students,
even the ones that irritated me,
will and cymone didn't irritate me,
    they were beautiful—

3

it was 2004
    and i loved cymone,
and i loved will,
cymone was a masterful writer with a
    sharp wit,
will was a masterful actor with
    impeccable timing,
two brilliant and beautiful and Black
    young people,
i invited others to see how beautiful they were,
    isn't that what an ode is?
    a veneration of something?
will starred in a children's play his
    class produced,
audience after audience howled at his
    portrayal of a bumbling and villainous king,
(an inspired take on our school principal
    a white principal,
    less john keats, more mr. rooney),
cymone's brilliance was more gut-wrenching,
    see:

4

it was 2004 and
    another Black person was murdered by the police,
this happened near cymone's house,
    happened before george floyd,
    will happen after george floyd,
    in the same city,
minneapolis is my home,
    it's cymone's and will's home too,
cymone wrote a poem about it,
    a fucking electric poem,
i invited her to read this poem to

all of my english classes,
  9th grade english,
  11th grade composition,
i wanted them to hear cymone's poem,
i got her excused from the rest of her
  classes that day,
so everyone could see cymone the poet,
a brilliant and beautiful and Black
  poet,
cymone answered questions after
  reading her poem,
the atmosphere in class was electric,
  such a vital day in school
i don't have the transcripts, so i guess
  you'll just have to trust my memory,
my memories reminds me that is was
  a good day—

5

i googled cymone and will
  when i started to write this poem,
cymone is a lawyer,
will is an empty facebook page,
i don't really know what happened to them
  after 2004,
i don't really know what happened to me
  after 2004,
keeps happening to me after 2004,
i do know that i wrote an email to cymone
  after writing this poem,
i wanted to tell cymone about my poem,
  i shared a draft with cymone in 2022,
  like the draft she shared in 2004,
cymone replied,
here's what she wrote:
  i absolutely remember that poem,
  i performed it at the talent show,
  you asked me to come read it to all of your english classes,
  i am super humbled to hear that you're
    writing and thinking about it all these years later,
  i was so nervous to perform it at the talent show back then,
  you really made me all the more confident in my writing,
  i have carried that with me til this day,
  the enthusiasm you showed up to class with everyday,
    coupled with the way you pushed us to think outside of the box,
  made you an amazing teacher back then,
    I can only imagine how great of a professor you are now—

ode to cymone and will (ode is a really white, really funny word) • 89

i've given up seeking
    validation as a teacher,
"you're my favorite teacher,"
"you're amazing,"
    etc.,
still, i know that exchanging emails with cymone
    felt good,
she still seemed so brilliant and beautiful,
and i know that brilliant and beautiful
    are often at odds with school,
and i know that Black
    is often at odds with school,
and i know that odes aren't at odds with school,
at best these last three lines i just wrote are
    funny,
at worst they are sinful,
here's what i don't know:
    whether or not this poem is an ode—

6

so please don't think this poem is about me,
another good white teacher trying to
    show how good they are to Black people,
desperately seeking the approval of
    Black people,
desperately trying to show off what a good
    white person i am,
this poem isn't about the tropes of white people
    always working out their whiteness,
    ode to me, ode to mine,
no, this poem is about what a beautiful day of school we shared
    when cymone came and gave readings,
    when cymone's words bounced off the walls,
    when cymone electrified the space,
and this is about how much his friends enjoyed it
    when will lurched on stage in a crown,
    when will furrowed his brow,
    when will impersonated the principal,
beautiful young people doing beautiful strange things,
and part of love might be providing strange spaces for
    people to be beautiful,
and part of school ought to provide strange spaces for
    young people to be beautiful—

7

white supremacy gets in the way,
    way of love,

way of beauty,
way of brilliance,
white supremacy got in our way
cymone's way,
will's way,
my way,
white supremacy damages me,
white supremacy gets in the way
of my ability to connect with others
to connect with difference,
to love and to be loved,
white supremacy is a special kind of
witchcraft,
so let this be my poor attempt at an
ode to cymone and will,
ode to strange moments in school,
a veneration of the day when
cymone was a celebrated poet,
will was a celebrated actor,
and we were together in a classroom
grinning, laughing, and weeping
at beautiful people doing
strange and beautiful things,
beautiful people sharing a beautiful moment
despite school,
seeking a love that is stronger than
white supremacy,
seeking a love that is stronger than
witchcraft—

CHAPTER 11

DEFINING "BELONGING" IN CLASSROOMS

Collected Narratives From Two Educators in Art and Science at Higher Education Institutions

Kyungeun Lim
Kennesaw State University

Soon Goo Lee
University of North Carolina Wilmington

INTRODUCTION

"Where are you from? What brought you here?" These are common questions for people who have immigrated to new locations. We, Asian American scholars, have been asked these questions from a variety of places, including classrooms, and thus the issue of "belonging and identity" has always been a major topic that we have been thinking about and pondering in our lives as immigrants. The process of answering questions "how can educators redefine belonging for students who are Black, Indigenous, and People Of Color (BIPOC)?" and "how do university educators respond to the topic of belonging in higher education especially in the classroom?" is also an extension of finding answers to the questions we have asked.

We received our K–12 and college education abroad but completed our doctoral degrees in the United States. Meaning we have spent over 12 and 16 years, respectively, in higher education in the United States. Currently, as educators and researchers, we teach college students at higher education institutions located in the United States and conduct academic research in the fields of art education and biochemistry. While exploring common themes in STEAM and how to bring them into the classroom, we have discussed how educators from nondominant cultures can construct classrooms of American universities for students from diverse ethnic groups and cultures can feel belonging. Through our long journey to find the most appropriate compromises and solutions, we have confronted several challenges that required us to redefine our identities as Asian American scholars. By sharing our stories, we hope readers will learn how educators come to shape their identities and how to effectively encourage student belonging in learning communities. As effective methods to deliver our stories, this chapter utilizes microhistorical perspectives and collective narrative methods to discuss virtual reality (VR)-mediated STEAM curriculum.

OUR STORIES

The Art Educator's Story

Lim completed her K–16 education in an East Asian country and received her doctoral degree in art education and education policy studies in the United States. Although she had been living in the United States for over a decade and working as an active art educator and researcher in her professional and academic fields, it was still an interesting experience for her being the only Asian American in her classroom setting. She described this experience as "interesting" because being racially isolated in a classroom environment can feel uncomfortable. As the sole foreign doctoral student and instructor in classes for many years, she found that her colleagues and students wondered how and why she had come to the United States. In a more extreme case, while teaching as an instructor, she encountered a few students who looked at her curiously and hesitated to communicate with her, seeming to think that "the foreign instructor" did not speak English. After a few experiences, she realized that sharing her stories could empower many students and broaden their understanding of belonging.

The Science Educator's Story

Lee believes that science is a universal language for communicating with students from diverse cultural, ethnic, and educational backgrounds. Since 2008, he has taken every opportunity to share his knowledge with graduate and undergraduate students in the laboratory. In many cases, students have been highly motivated but faced different challenges in becoming active members of his research group. For example, an undergraduate student who was born and raised in Japan tended to avoid taking initiative in group discussions. Likewise, another undergraduate, a second-generation immigrant and a Minority Access to Research Careers (MARC) Undergraduate Student Training in Academic Research (U*STAR) scholar, often lacked confidence even though her work generated high-quality data. For both students, major turning points were the successful outcomes of their independent research projects. Their research achievements made them participate in research with greater enthusiasm and feel more belonging in the research community. His students have not only conducted small- and large-scale independent research projects but have also become authors of peer-reviewed research papers. Thus, he believes that science is an effective solution for breaking down hidden barriers, such as language and culture, and the ownership of projects facilitates this barrier-breaking process.

OUR VOICES AS MICROHISTORY

Let's think about history first. Can ordinary people be included in mainstream history, macrohistory, in the realm of history learning? What does it mean to listen to the life stories of ordinary people? Regarding these questions, we have been inspired by microhistory research perspective (Brewer, 2010). In the movement of reconsideration of BIPOC, the voices of ordinary people would contain in-depth relationships and thoughts (Brewer, 2010, p. 2). Unlike macro-history, which focuses on major historical events or only a small number of people with historical significance, microhistory "capture[s] the drama of everyday life. They let readers understand people as agents of change for the worlds they live in, often in the face of overwhelming difficulties" (A Humanities Unbounded Collaborative Project in History at Duke University, n.d.). In addition, microhistorical perspectives, it helps to collect hidden voices to convey realistic history. Renders and De Haan (2014) explained the meaning of microhistory could "expose hidden structures and produce ample documentation of aspects of life normally kept in silence" (Renders & De Haan, 2014, p. 110). The significance of microhistorical perspective in research is its connection with qualitative research and collective narratives, as it can be used to collect thick descriptions (Sweet, 2021). As part of the process of understanding these perspectives and introducing them into our classrooms, in the following section we discuss how we adopted this qualitative research method and our experiences with the collective narrative approach.

COLLECTIVE NARRATIVES: STORYTELLING

The purpose of collecting narratives is to understand situations that are specific to cultures and increase contextual understanding (Garvis, 2015). Narratives as stories are critical sources for qualitative research (Merriam, 2009; Shevellar, 2015). Merriam (2009) pointed out that the first-person voice could effectively deliver live experiences and meanings. Thus, researchers have utilized collective narratives and narrative analysis, giving significant consideration to narratives in qualitative studies.

Regarding the narratives of people of color, various studies have centered their voices (Jang, 2017; Rodríguez & Greer, 2017). Rodríguez and Greer (2017) utilized collective counternarratives to understand the educational experiences of students of color. They collected and tracked participants' stories and found similarities and differences to draw the educational landscape for students in similar situations. Jang (2017) shared an autobiographical story about his scholarly identity and the challenges he faced as a minority faculty member in higher education. He argued that scholars from underrepresented groups had a responsibility to share stories and cross-cultural experiences to resist stereotyping in academia.

Readers may wonder what they get from hearing other people's stories. As discussed earlier, narratives and stories can help increase contextual understanding and lived experiences. Atkinson and Mitchell (2010) explained the strengths of narrative research. They recognized how the same story could be read differently by readers through a process of interpretation based on the readers' previous experiences. They suggested that researchers consider the fact that readers may understand stories differently by reconstructing their own meanings and stories. Like Atkinson and Mitchell, we also invite readers to interpret and reconstruct stories based on their experiences.

Case One: Building Classrooms for Belonging with Online Resources and Technologies

The first activity took place in the fall semester of 2021 at a public university located in the southwestern United States. The class aim was to introduce and practice various research topics in art education, especially arts integration, STEAM, and digitally engaged learning, primarily for undergraduate students majoring in art education.

The Setting

For this project, the first author (i.e., art educator) mainly led the classes, and the second author (i.e., science educator) jointly developed the curriculum content and taught the second session. The materials required were virtual reality (VR) devices and publicly available online resources, such as Google Earth Pro (Google LLC.).

The activity consisted of five 75-minute sessions that were taught in either in-person or hybrid delivery modality (see Figure 11.1). The aim of the first session was to understand the concept of arts integration and STEAM. Prior to the in-class activity, the primary instructor introduced the latest research and lesson examples related to arts integration and STEAM in a 75-minute pre-lecture. In the second session, the second instructor delivered a lecture on real science knowledge in the STEAM approach to students through both in-person and hybrid delivery modal-

Defining "Belonging" in Classrooms • 95

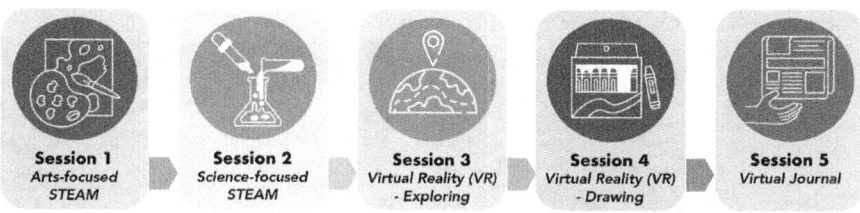

FIGURE 11.1. Five Stages of STEAM Lessons: Arts-Focused STEAM, Science-Focused STEAM, VR Exploring, VR Drawing, and Virtual Journal

ity. We designed this lesson for students to experience belonging as well as arts integration and STEAM. The session included a short 40-minute lecture, then we explained how to use Google Earth Pro, an easy-to-access software. Students were free to explore several places through Google Earth Pro after which they picked one cultural/historical site that was personally meaningful to them (see Figure 11.2). Students visited the university's VR studio and virtually explored the meaningful places they had chosen and practiced using VR applications, especially drawing tools. In the fourth session, most of the students expressed their interest in VR drawing tools and individually revisited the VR studio to complete the final project by turning their learning and experiences into a visual journal with visual presentations.

Belonging and Diversity

The goal of the in-class activity was to enable students to explore and visualize their own personal histories and share them with other classmates. In the class-

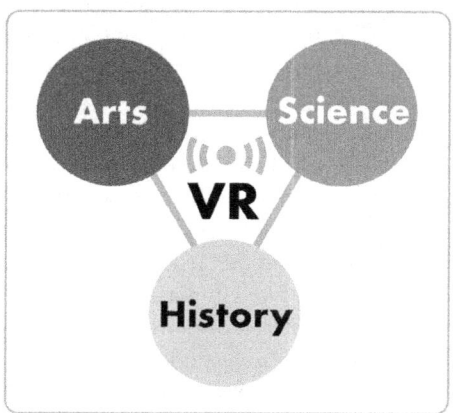

FIGURE 11.2. Arts-Integrated Subjects: These Lessons Integrated Arts, Science, and History With VR.

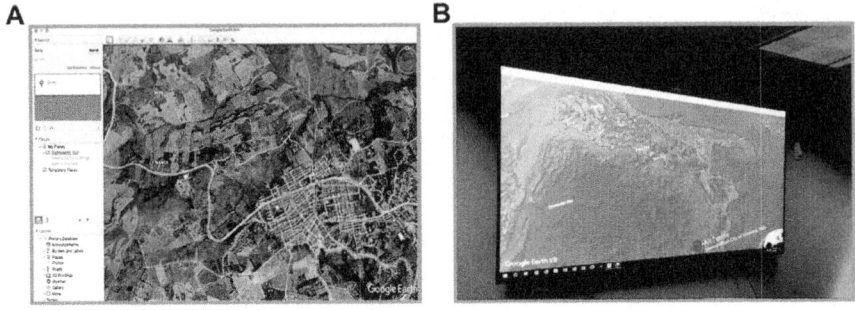

FIGURE 11.3. Google Earth: A Student Visited Sicily via Google Earth Pro (A) and VR Google Earth (B).

room, 18 undergraduate students with diverse cultural and ethnic backgrounds, White, Native American, and Indigenous students, actively participated in the five sessions. Based on student feedback and class evaluations, we believe this integrated activity allowed students to more deeply understand their inner selves and to reflect and express their personal histories through the easy-to-access and newly emerging scientific technologies.

One student took a virtual visit to Sicily in Italy using both Google Earth Pro on a personal computer and the Google Earth app on a VR device. As shown in Figure 11.3, the student visited a historical site that was personally meaningful to her and tracked the history of the place using a VR device and the Time Slider function in Google Earth Pro. Since the Time Slider enables users to see time-lapse videos and historical imagery of specific locations, students could change the time of a location's images by using a bar on the top. This student explained that her grandparents and entire extended family had come to the United States from Sicily in the early 1920s. In her class presentation, she stated: "I don't think I am an Italian now, but I always wonder about the place where my roots came from. That's why I chose this place."

Another story came from a student who was from an Indigenous reservation in the southwestern United States. Through the VR device and Google Earth Pro, the student visited and captured images of her home and neighbors. Furthermore, she also explained in her presentation why she took this integrated course and that she wanted to become a well-trained teacher, which she related to her ethnic and cultural roots in her presentations. Importantly, through teacher education at this higher education institution, she said she wanted to support the community in which she had grown up and to improve students' learning back home.

In summary, throughout the integrated education sessions focusing on microhistory and using technology, our students were able to expand their understanding of new technologies and visualize their inner and personal experiences through the process of giving and receiving feedback. The processes encouraged students to express themselves to others and practice listening to other's stories visually and verbally. "I feel I know more about others in this classroom now. I know their stories, I know who they are, where they are from, and I know what they are interested in now" (Student's reflection, 2021). As a student mentioned above, many of the participating students found novel approaches to share both positive and negative experiences from their diverse cultural and ethnic backgrounds and to set a macroscopic direction for how to solve their past and current issues in the future.

Case Two: Curriculum for Improving the Experience of Marginalized Students in Art and Science Education

In Case One, we discussed novel methods for constructing a classroom where students can comfortably share their inner stories related to identity and introduced effective new online resources and technologies. The story of Case Two now focuses on how we have been able to utilize the same set of resources for marginalized students, in particular, to improve their sense of belonging in the school community and in multiple disciplines from the perspective of BIPOC.

The Setting

In the fields of science and science education, there is educational inequality (Bair & Bair, 2010). For example, Rifkin (2020) reported on the racial identification of U.S. physicists and astronomers. In 2017, 59.2% of physicists and astronomers were White, 32.7% were Asian, 4.1% were Hispanic/Latinx, 3.9% were Black, and 0% were Native American/Pacific Islander. Besides the academic scholar population, K–12 students have also experienced inequality in their science education through limitations in science resources and opportunities (Bair & Bair, 2010).

Considering this, the purpose of the second project was to expand opportunities to experience STEAM to local students from marginalized backgrounds. The science outreach activity was conducted in the summer of 2019 in local communities near a public state university located in the southeastern United States. The activity was a 150-minute (2.5-hour) program for local marginalized secondary students. The program consisted of five sessions: (1) basic lecture on science, (2) art workshop with science, (3) programming graphic rendering software to construct 3D protein structures, (4) exploring 3D protein structures with VR, and (5) presenting and sharing reflections and emotions. Participants were 24 students aged 16–18 years, and their races and ethnicities were Latinx, Black, Asian, and White.

In the basic lecture on science (30 minutes), the second author, a science educator and researcher, taught the basics concepts and principles of biochemistry in an easy-to-understand manner, emphasizing proteins and their 3D structures. In the following session (30 minutes), the first author, an art educator and researcher, held a short workshop called Art Workshop with Science that introduced how art

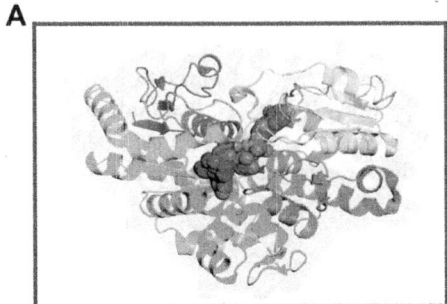 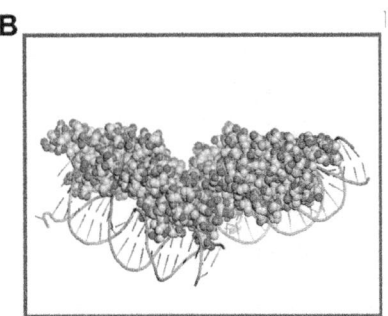

FIGURE 11.4. Instructors' Sample Artworks: Students Also Expressed 3D Molecular Protein Structures and Added Artistic Touches Using PyMOL (Schrödinger).

and science have been grafted into the art field. As a core activity in the second session, students utilized conventional art expression techniques and materials to make creative art on science, especially proteins, using their newly acquired knowledge from the previous lecture.

In the third session, on programming graphic rendering software, students learned how to use PyMOL (Schrödinger, INC.), which scientists use to visualize molecules and that is free, in a computer laboratory located in the university library. Each student had opportunities to appreciate existing renderings of 3D molecular protein structures, reconstruct molecules using graphic editing tools, and finally create professionally rendered images (see Figure 11.4).

In the following session, VR devices allowed students to immersively explore the 3D protein structures that they had used in the second and third sessions with Nanome (Nanome, Inc), a VR application originally developed for structural biologists, medicinal chemists, and computational chemists, that displays proteins and small molecules in VR space from various angles. Finally, in the fifth session, similar to the session in Case One during which students made virtual journals with visual presentations, students wrote a short reflection paper to describe their experiences and exhibited the artwork they created using conventional methods (second session) and the graphically rendered structures from PyMOL (third session) to their parents and community members.

Sharing the Belief That "I Can Do It"

We designed this activity to improve students' learning motivation and expand their opportunities to experience science and technology tools. The outcome of our efforts to confront inequality in scientific/artistic integration experiences can be found in students' final reflection papers. For example, a female Hispanic student commented on her experiences:

> I have not used VR before. This lesson helps me to think out of the box. Now, I can know there are things beyond boring science textbooks.

Each student had the opportunity to give a presentation and share their artwork over the five sessions. Specifically, after creating art in the artistic workshop, students displayed their integrated science artwork and had a gallery walk to explain their work and share what they had learned from each session. In addition, students had a second presentation and sharing time in the VR session. Consequently, the students were able to share their stories with other students in the classroom as well as their parents and community members in the final presentation session. A Black male student's comments in his reflection paper were especially inspiring:

> Although I am here to take STEAM classes, I have not jumped into the STEM subjects well. But today's class make me think about science differently. It could go with art or games! I feel I am more confident in doing science or math now. I feel I can do them and want to try to study them more.

In the same vein, we believe this series of sessions delivers a meaningful message to teachers who teach marginalized education populations, including BIPOC students. Since the participating students were of the first generation to be raised tech-savvy in visual media and with a high percentage of visual learners, we actively introduced new technology to convey complex scientific knowledge as part of our teaching methodology (Lee et al., 2020). Leveraging educational versions of software such as PyMOL and Nanome, we were able to offer the students a chance to graphically and virtually explore science content that is difficult to understand intuitively. This helped them realistically examine molecular features and touch them virtually, leading to enhanced understanding. The following sections describe what motivated us to design the art and science integration curriculum and what we experience as BIPOC in academia.

OUR STORIES AGAIN

The Art Educator's Story

In Case One, Lim tried to answer the following questions: How can students share their stories with others comfortably and creatively? What are the best ways to express their stories visually? How can technology and science help students' storytelling? With the storytelling, how can students feel emotionally connected to other students in the classroom? In answer to these questions, she collaborated with a scientist and began to integrate science and technology. In particular, she observed emerging technologies, especially VR, helped students connect more deeply in two ways. First, students were able to understand others' stories more realistically and closely through visual images accompanied by written and spoken text. Second, students naturally began to build cooperative relationships through learning new skills and tools. The process of talking and cooperating made them feel more comfortable talking about their own stories and more of a sense of belonging to the learning community.

The Science Educator's Story

The most amazing discovery in his comparative studies of proteins structures has been that many proteins in evolutionarily diverse organisms have maintained almost identical structures for 600–1,200 million years at the atomic level. Just as each gene is differently expressed and functions depending on a variety of environmental cues, people can develop and express themselves in various ways. Lee firmly believes that education is one of the most important environmental factors there are to encourage an individual's limitless intellectual capacity. As a leader of a research group and an educator in higher education, he has created educational opportunities and has pursued educational equity in the laboratory, in the classroom, and in the greater university community.

His long-term goal in education is sharing scientific knowledge to increase scientific literacy in traditionally marginalized groups in his community. As shown in Case Two, he believes the science outreach programs in his local community can attract younger students, who are familiar with visual media but have not experienced science activities, to science. As an educator, he has designed and provided various education programs making science more accessible to disadvantaged students to boost their interest in science.

MOVING FORWARD

Let's go back to our opening questions from the introduction. In this chapter, we have shared two curriculum designs that leverage STEAM approaches to answer the question of how to include diverse students' identities and encourage belonging. The first curriculum (Case One) enabled students to feel a sense of belonging to their learning communities, allowing them to speak about and express their diverse identities and ethnic backgrounds. The second curriculum (Case Two) focused on expanding educational opportunities, and empowered students and increased learning motivation by allowing them to share their emotions with others. This process is meaningful to BIPOC students who have been alienated in the STEAM domain.

How were our personal stories? Did our stories convey meaningful historical moments? As of Spring 2022, at the time of writing this chapter, BIPOC and anti-Asian issues have become more significant than before to Asian Americans, including those who studied at and have been teaching at higher education institutions in the United States. Through the microhistorical lens, our stories are able to provide vivid experiences and open discussions of "small places intensively these historians discovered facts that were often unknown to participants and invisible to earlier scholarship" (Brown, 2003, pp. 10-11). These stories, like us, have not been considered in the mainstream of history. In line with Jang (2017), we felt it was our responsibility to tell our stories and make our voices heard to help promote inclusion, diversity, and awareness of BIPOC issues. With our stories of why and how we designed these curriculums in relation to our identities and histories, we hope more educators from underrepresented populations speak out and share their stories.

REFERENCES

Atkinson, B., & Mitchell, R. (2010). "Why didn't they get it?" "Did they have to get it?": What reader response theory has to offer narrative research and pedagogy. *International Journal of Education & the Arts, 11*(7), 1–25.

Bair, M. A., & Bair, D. (2010). Scheduling inequality in math and science: How trimesters hurt students at risk of academic failure. *American Secondary Education, 39*(1), 78–94.

Brewer, J. (2010). Microhistory and the histories of everyday life. *Cultural and Social History, 7*(1), 87–109.

Brown, R. (2003). Microhistory and post-modern challenge. *Journal of the Early Republic, 23*(1), 1–20.

Garvis, S. (2015). *Narrative constellations: Exploring lived experience in education.* Brill.

A Humanities Unbounded Collaborative Project in History at Duke University. (no date). *What is microhistory?* https://sites.duke.edu/microworldslab/what-is-microhistory/

Jang, B. G. (2017). Am I a qualified literacy researcher and educator? A counter-story of a professional journey of one Asian male literacy scholar in the United States. *Journal of Literacy Research, 49*(4), 559–581.

Lee, S. G., Fleming, J., & Fritzler, P. (2020). Digital makerspace for chemical education. In J. Hicks & J. Long, J. (Eds.), *Makerspaces for adults: Best practices and great projects* (pp. 159–165). Rowman & Littlefield.

Merriam, S. (2009). *Qualitative research: A guide to design and implementation.* Wiley & Sons.

Renders, H., & De Haan, B. (2014). *Theoretical discussions of biography: Approaches from history, microhistory, and life writing* (Rev. and augmented ed.). Brill.

Rifkin, M. (2020). Who does science? Using data to explore society, inequality, and social justice in the context of science. *Science Teacher, 87*(9), 24–31.

Rodríguez, L. F., & Greer, W. (2017). (Un)Expected scholars: Counter-narratives from two (boys) men of color across the educational pipeline. *Equity & Excellence in Education, 50*(1), 108–120.

Shevellar, L. (2015). From bearers of problems to bearers of culture: Developing community in the community development classroom. *International Journal of Qualitative Studies in Education (QSE), 28*(4), 457–475.

Sweet, J. A. (2021). Making history come alive: The Boston Massacre trials. *History Teacher, 54*(3), 509–538.

CHAPTER 12

CENTERING ASIAN WOMEN'S FEMINIST ANGER USING ZINES IN ART EDUCATION

Eunkyung Hwang
Pennsylvania State University

Popular culture in the United States has distorted Asian women's anger as apolitical anger and rendered Asian women invisible even though their anger against anti-Asian racism has the potential to resist the nation's racialized landscape. In this chapter, I claim that art educators should focus on Asian women's feminist anger (Kay & Banet-Weiser, 2019) and the efficacy of using zines in art education by questioning the erasure of Asian women's anger. Using a contemporary comic zine *Koreangry* (Jeong, 2019) and a pedagogy of discomfort (Boler, 1999; Zembylas, 2007), art educators can facilitate students' collective witnessing of Asian American women's lived experiences and suffering and help them challenge the prevalent racial biases and discriminations against Asian women in the U.S. society. Students will be able to realize their ethical responsibilities toward social justice and ultimately reconstruct counter-narratives towards racial solidarity through their zine-making.

In recent years the political expression of women's anger, an expression exemplified by the #MeToo movement[1] starting from 2017, has swept through the world

---

[1] #Metoo Movement is a feminist social movement against normalized sexual abuse that publicizes people's experiences of sexual harassment in all industries (Kay & Banet-Weiser, 2019).

BIPOC Alliances: Building Communities and Curricula, pages 103–113.
Copyright © 2023 by Information Age Publishing
www.infoagepub.com
All rights of reproduction in any form reserved.

(Kay & Banet-Weiser, 2019). This emergence of women's anger brings necessary attention to how the U.S. and other Eurocentric societies have treated such anger as taboo, while also demonstrating how the collective power of women's anger can change the political landscape and threaten societal oppression (Orgad & Gill, 2019). However, the anger of Asian women has still been relatively silenced, with various populations continuing to be dismissed as emotionally inexpressive based on racialized expectations of a subordinate femininity. As an Asian woman art educator in a White dominant college town in the U.S., my daily life is replete with references to me and other Asians as *hardworking people,* others' active avoidance in public spaces, and even at times we're labeled as *potential COVID-19 spreaders*. Instead of responding angrily to these racial microaggressions, I find myself concealing the anger. I cannot but respond nicely to prove myself a *civilized* Asian woman who fits the stereotype of a model minority.[2] Even worse, the social-emotional learning (SEL) paradigm in U.S. education, including art education, has only underscored the importance of controlling anger regardless of the political value of marginalized people's anger towards social transformation. This pathologization of anger leaves me with this question: How should art educators counter the racialized erasure of Asian women's anger through art education praxis?

To answer the question, this chapter looks at the pedagogical possibilities of centering collective witnessing of feminist anger (Kay & Banet-Weiser, 2019) against Anti-Asian racism using zines in art education. I examine the distortion and erasure of Asian women's anger in education and society. Based on my positionality as an Asian woman art educator, I highlight the need to center Asian women's feminist anger by using a pedagogy of discomfort (Boler, 1999; Zembylas, 2007). Zines can be a great pedagogical avenue offering students various counter-narratives of Asian women's feminist anger and inquiry into such anger. The contemporary comic zine *Koreangry* is one pedagogical medium that shows feminist anger of Korean immigrant women. I aim to offer pedagogical insight to art educators who seek to dismantle racialized depictions of women's anger and illuminate their potential in education praxis. This chapter ultimately seeks to build solidarity towards racial justice with students through centering Asian women's lived experiences.

RE-INTERPRETATION OF ASIAN WOMEN'S ANGER AS FEMINIST ANGER

Since the days of Aristotle, Eurocentric society has operated on a reason/emotion binary, a framework on human psychology that claims that reason is humanity's only means of self-control. Only recently has there been any pushback in defense

---

[2] Model minority is a stereotype of Asian Americans in U.S. society. The stereotype universally frames Asian Americans as socio-economic high achievers who are obedient to White dominant cultural values unlike other racial minorities. The myth of model minority has reinforced misconceptions that Asian Americans do not face any racial challenges and has justified the exclusion of Asian Americans in social discourse about racial justice (Iftikar & Museus, 2018).

of anger, which is normally repressed (Stenberg, 2011). Anger, a strong emotion of being upset, has historically been regarded as dangerous since it threatens rationality—and, critically, the established structure of society (Kay & Banet-Weiser, 2019). Several decades ago, however, various academic disciplines began to study anger as positive: Anger can motivate people to engage in politics (Thompson, 2006), self-reflect (Zembylas, 2007), and collectively respond to shared problems in their community (Hogan, 2020). Unfortunately, this new respect for anger has not extended beyond these few academic disciplines.

Despite recent acknowledgement that anger can be an important part of societal growth, that acknowledgement remains dependent on one's positionality within larger societal power structures, such as race and gender (Holmes, 2004). Regarding race, Phoenix (2019) notes that Black anger has been historically demonized as a defiant behavior while White anger has been legitimized and championed as a justifiable political action. In addition to the racialization of anger, U.S. society has continuously pathologized women's anger as a loss of control but tolerates men's anger as a natural feature of masculinity (Kim, 2011). Often, sexist interpretations of anger continue to intersect with racism in ways that stigmatize women of color and their anger. The hypervisibility of Black and Latina women's anger portraying Black and Brown women as hostile and intellectually inferior paradoxically conceals the cause of that anger—namely, the intergenerational trauma of racial and gender discrimination in global society (Collins, 1990; Griffin, 2012; Mora, 2018). Women of color have had to suppress their anger so as not to be defined by the rampant stereotype of an angry Black woman or a spicy Latina (Mora, 2018; Phoenix, 2019).

Instead of being depicted as wild, Asian women have been stereotyped as demure, rarely expressing anger (Fang, 2021). This distorted idea of Asian women has produced the trope of "ornamental Asiatic femininity" (Cheng, 2019, p. 23) in the media, a fetishization of Asian women as decorative objects without agency. Through this dehumanization of Asian women, U.S. popular culture has diminished the political role of Asian women's anger, limiting its effect against racial discrimination and reproduced images of depoliticized anger. The angry Asian girl and tiger mother tropes are compelling examples of the racialized objectification of Asian women's anger which reduce Asian women's anger to something completely ineffectual or only domestically effective. The former is a cutified version of unaggressive anger, the latter is a mother who forces her children to academically succeed (Cheng, 2019; Rhee, 2013). These tropes demonstrate how even when Asian women's anger is acknowledged in popular culture, it still stereotypes an Asian femininity in which Asian women are not capable agents of change for undermining the patriarchal society.

Feminist scholars have defended the value of women's anger and highlighted the productive role of women's anger against societal oppressions. Audre Lorde (1997) highlights women of color's anger against White supremacy since it can translate their suffering into knowledge and political action aiming to open a more equitable future. Anger, for Lorde, is a source of empowerment and liberation rather than merely destructive fury. She claims that we should learn to use anger as a source of strength in our daily lives. Sara Ahmed (2009) also illuminates that women's anger is crucial energy that enables women to resist racism and sexism. Even when the anger has been dismissed as killjoy behavior that destroys the mood, she claims, feminists should speak out the anger and willfully become "killjoy feminists" (p. 48) to open an equitable world. Additionally, Jilly Boyce Kay and Sarah Banet-Weiser (2019) refer to women's political anger as feminist anger that can dismantle systemic oppressions and inequality. Their definition of feminist anger does not limit representations of anger as solely from those who self-identify as feminists; rather, theirs is a feminist interpretation of the potential effect of women's political anger to elucidate how systemic oppressions work. Based on these works, educators can reinterpret Asian women's anger against anti-Asian racism as the energizing force of feminist anger, a productive impetus toward racial justice rather than apolitical anger.

PEDAGOGY OF DISCOMFORT AND CRITICAL EMOTIONAL PRAXIS IN ART EDUCATION

Armed with the goal of using feminist anger as an agent of social change, art educators must seek educational models allowing students to realize the value of such anger. Megan Boler (1999) suggests "pedagogy of discomfort" as a practice engaging the "discomforting process of questioning cherished beliefs and assumptions" (p. 176). Boler defines bearing witness as a testimonial reading that requires students' active participation and responsibility. Through collective witnessing, students can do critical inquiry about the way they perceive others' emotions and eventually understand the importance of mutual responsibility for social transformation. Advocating Boler's pedagogy, Michalinos Zembylas (2007) further claims that educators should embrace "ambivalent anger" (p. 24) that cannot be simply dichotomized as positive or negative. Such an approach supports students' recognition of others' suffering and negotiation of the definition of anger; in turn, students might perceive anger as a positive force that helps to construct critical conversation and enact meaningful social changes (Zembylas, 2007).

Despite this compelling research regarding emotion-related pedagogy, the productive role of women of color's feminist anger is still understudied in art education. Art education researchers instead have focused on the educational potential of critical emotional praxis examining the collective and political role of various emotions (Zembylas, 2007). Kwon's research (2020), for example, shows how the pedagogy of discomfort in art education can help students critically understand their emotions and acknowledge how the reason/emotion dichotomy in Western epistemology undervalues the role of emotion. She asserts that art educators can empower marginalized women by facilitating engagement with their emotions and lived experiences. In sum, the critical examination of feminist anger through the pedagogy of discomfort can open new avenues for students' active inquiry into anger as a driver of change.

COLLECTIVE WITNESSING OF ASIAN WOMEN'S FEMINIST ANGER USING ZINES

Regarding this scarcity of art education research focusing on feminist anger, how should art educators center Asian women's feminist anger in education praxis? I suggest using collective witnessing as highlighted by Boler (1999) and Zembylas (2007). Students' explorations of visual works that challenge their values and prior experience through counter-narratives can be the collective witnessing in art education. Art educators should facilitate this exploration for students to uncover the productive role of anger in various narratives and encourage students to reflect on where that anger comes from and where their own anger most commonly comes from. Such counter-narratives will challenge students' cultural norms, creating empathy where there was ignorance.

Utilizing zines as pedagogical sites is one of the promising ways for art educators to cultivate students' collective witnessing of feminist anger. Independently published, zines are short magazines that deal with community specific knowledge and are created and distributed by the communities themselves (Congdon & Blandy, 2003). As part of civil disobedience movements beginning in 1970s, zines often include voices from marginalized communities, giving their collective experience a platform (Duncombe, 1997). Zines challenge dominant narratives of cultural representation and discuss societal oppressions in a frank manner (Piepmeier, 2009). Accordingly, zines are a great avenue for students to explore marginalized women's experiences (Weida, 2013). Accordingly, art educators should center zines with marginalized women's experiences to facilitate students' active explorations of feminist anger, validate their personal experiences, and develop their critical thinking skills (Creasap, 2014; Weida, 2013). Most critically, unlike many other modes of social justice awareness development through art, zines are an accessible form of self-expression that students can readily participate in. Zine-making activities can further inspire students to collectively reflect through creativity and challenge their audiences to dismantle dominant ideologies and build solidarity among marginalized people (Desyllas & Sinclair, 2014).

Through the collective witnessing of Asian women's feminist anger in zines, and the subsequent building of students' own zines, students can engage with their emotional responses to Asian women's anger and suffering. Students will gradually participate in critical conversation with their colleagues, question their racial and gender biases against Asian women, and internalize new knowledge of this anger and its historical marginalization. Educators should note that this collective witnessing must not lead to a simple assumption or a self-complacent empathy about Asian women's experiences. Instead, students should first acknowledge that their own identities and beliefs exist in relation to others and society, and that their identities are flexible (Boler, 1999). After constructing an in-depth understanding of students' positionalities, educators should increase students' sense of "vigilance" to be attentive to Asian women's anger and build solidarity with them (Zembylas, 2007, p. 26). This vigilance will help students to further understand various oppressions that Asian women are facing and to create their own zines regarding racial and gender equality. In the process, students can actively investigate the anger of other marginalized populations and seek ways to make that anger visible to the society in a way that empowers both themselves and marginalized people. This attempt can be motivation for students to create their own zines while finding the answers and eventually lead students to resist White patriarchal society.

Granted, questioning one's fundamental values and beliefs is not easy. In the process, students might encounter feelings of guilt and intensified discomfort such as defensive anger. Art educators should assure students that the art classroom is a safe place for diverse ambivalent feelings and honest reflection (Boler, 1999). Self-disclosure of one's positionalities and vulnerabilities will contribute to an atmosphere of respect through demonstration of the need for collective reflection. This culture of respect can help students realize how it feels to have their emotions respected, even those traditionally regarded as negative emotions like anger and discomfort. Students can eventually understand the importance of critical exploration of feminist anger and further allowing space for feminist anger. According to Piepmeier (2009), zines create "embodied communities" (p. 214) with an affectionate connection between zine artists and their readers, one that makes the desire for community building visible. Thus, emotional connections constructed through zines can create an emotionally supportive classroom. In the long term, these connections can prevent students' avoidance of responsibility to racial justice and facilitate students' attempts for social transformation (Guzzetti & Gamboa, 2004; Weida, 2013).

KOREANGRY: KOREAN AMERICAN WOMEN'S ANGER IN A COMIC ZINE

Koreangry is a contemporary comic zine by Asian American artist Eunsoo Jeong (2019). Jeong is a Korean immigrant who was undocumented for about a decade before receiving Deferred Action for Childhood Arrivals (DACA)[3] status. The main character is a 7-inch clay figure—Jeong's alter-ego—narrating feelings of being othered as an Asian American woman and criticizing societal oppressions in U.S. society. Koreangry shows its main character enduring various suffering due to racial fetishization and discrimination. Jeong humorously visualizes her "minor feelings"[4] (Hong, 2020, p. 56) using Koreangry's frowning faces and swear words. Leng (2020) claims that feminist humor is an activist tool that unsettles hegemonic ideologies and unravels social injustices. It can also persuade readers

---

[3] DACA is a form of legal permission that allows undocumented immigrants who entered the United States as minors to legally reside in the country to study or work. Although it deferred deportation of undocumented youth and young adults, it also failed to offer a pathway to legalization (Gonzales et al., 2014).

[4] The term minor feelings originates from the book Minor Feelings by Korean American writer Cathy Park Hong (2020). It refers to Asian Americans' complex emotions including frustration, depression, and resentment of being othered.

to joyfully take action towards social justice using their feminist anger. Accordingly, Koreangry's use of humor is a purposeful tactic to persuade readers' consciousness of feminist anger while they enjoy the catharsis of feminist humor. For example, using humorous words and body gestures, Jeong depicts the emotional burden of being an Asian woman who constantly feels pressure to fit into societal expectations (see Figure 12.1). While enjoying humor and bearing witness to the gendered and racialized expectations that fuel Koreangry's anger, students can learn to listen to feminist anger and engage in ongoing critical conversation about the power structure in U.S. society.

Rather than giving the main character a personal name, Jeong (2019) calls her Koreangry, the same as the zine's title. Given that Koreangry's experiences in the zine are directly relatable for many Asian women in contemporary U.S. society, we can look at Koreangry not only as an individual Asian American woman but also as a collective identity of Asian American women. Koreangry's furious expressions connect the racially marginalized women readers to their minor feelings and question the roles imposed upon Asian women by U.S. society. Accordingly,

FIGURE 12.1. Still Image of Koreangry #7 (Eunsoo Jeong, clay and digital image, 2019)

FIGURE 12.2. Still Image of Koreangry #9 (Eunsoo Jeong, clay and digital image, 2020)

the zine becomes a site where its creator's narratives and readers' lived experiences meet and construct an "embodied community" (Piepmeier, 2009, p. 214). This embodied experience enables students to further situate their self-identity in relation to White supremacist ideologies and patriarchal power structure actively at work in U.S. society.

The anger in Koreangry also shows that political anger enables marginalized people to build a coalitional foundation for collective liberation. Not solely focused on social justice issues related to anti-Asian racism, she highlights the need for solidarity among people of color and queer people by critically reflecting our own intersectional privileges. For instance, in emphasizing the need for a coalition of people of color in the Black Lives Matter movement[5] (see Figure 12.2), Koreangry addresses anti-Black racism that is deeply ingrained in people of color communities. In a letter to Korean Americans, Jeong (2020) bravely recounts the erased history of a racially motivated homicide committed by Korean American who fatally shot an African American girl in 1991.[6] She claims that the Korean American community should acknowledge that they are indebted to the civil rights movement of the 1960s and have benefited from racial privileges as Asian Americans within the systemic anti-Black racism that White supremacy has devised. This self-criticization through feminist anger can open new politi-

---

[5] Black Lives Matter is a social movement against racism and anti-Black violence, particularly criticizing police brutality in the U.S. (Lebron, 2017).

[6] In 1991, Soon Ja Du, a convenience-store owner, fatally shot Latasha Harlins, a 15-year-old Black girl who was walking away from her. Later, Du was sentenced to 5 years' probation, 400 hours of community service, a $500 restitution, and the payment of Harlins's funeral expenses—an extremely light sentence. This injustice became one of major causes of the 1992 Los Angeles uprising (Stevenson, 2013). Jeong acknowledges this homicide as an example of internalized anti-Black racism in the Asian American community.

cal discussions about interracial conflicts and internalized racial hierarchy in art classrooms. Also, Jeong's active engagement in her responsibility to uphold racial justice issues through the zine publication is an excellent example for students to learn that they must push beyond passive empathy or self-complacent reflection to transform our society's political landscape.

Admittedly, there is a risk that Koreangry will be dismissed as perpetuating cartoonish miniaturized anger—as a stereotype of Asian women's anger—since some readers might interpret the main character merely as cute. However, we should interpret Jeong's use of cuteness as a deliberate killjoy behavior that disrupt the stereotypes of depoliticized anger of cute young Asian women. While displaying Koreangry's counter-narrative as palatable and enjoyable with cuteness, the zine ultimately criticizes the stereotypes of Asian women's racialized femininity.

CONCLUSION

In this chapter, I highlighted the need for centering Asian women's feminist anger and the efficacy of using zines in art education. Questioning the erasure of Asian women's feminist anger—and showing alternatives to that erasure through zines—can challenge prevalent racial biases and discriminations in White dominant U.S. society. As a culmination of both the personal and collective feminist anger of Asian American women, Koreangry can facilitate students to collectively bear witness to Asian American women's suffering. Although the feminist anger in such zines cannot fully represent all Asian women's lived experiences, students at least can realize their ethical responsibility toward social justice by connecting their lived experiences and emotions with those in the zines; ultimately, they can imagine counter-narratives through an application of the pedagogy of discomfort and their own zine-making. Through genuine sharing of anger and vulnerabilities in art education with zines, art educators can encourage students to recognize the impacts of structural racism and sexism and support their active participation in critical conversations around social justice. I hope that centering Asian women's feminist anger in art education using zines will nourish students' commitment to dismantling societal oppressions through solidarity and increase their efficacy as active agents of social transformation.

REFERENCES

Ahmed, S. (2009). Embodying diversity: Problems and paradoxes for Black feminists. *Race Ethnicity and Education, 12*(1), 41–52.
Boler, M. (1999). *Feeling power: Emotions and education*. Routledge.
Cheng, A. A. (2019). *Ornamentalism*. Oxford University Press.
Collins, P. H. (1990). Black feminist thought in the matrix of domination. *Black feminist thought: Knowledge, consciousness, and the politics of empowerment, 138*(1990), 221–238.

Congdon, K. G., & Blandy, D. (2003). Zinesters in the classroom: Using zines to teach about postmodernism and the communication of ideas. *Art Education, 56*(3), 44–55.

Creasap, K. (2014). Zine-making as feminist pedagogy. *Feminist Teacher, 24*(3), 155–168.

Desyllas, M. C., & Sinclair, A. (2014). Zine-Making as a pedagogical tool for transformative learning in social work education. *Social Work Education, 33*(3), 296–316.

Duncombe, S. (1997). *Notes from underground: Zines and the politics of alternative culture*. Verso.

Fang, N. (2021). The aggressive potential and yellow anger. *Psychoanalysis, Culture & Society, 26*(4), 561–578.

Gonzales, R. G., Terriquez, V., & Ruszczyk, S. P. (2014). Becoming DACAmented: Assessing the short-term benefits of deferred action for childhood arrivals (DACA). *American Behavioral Scientist, 58*(14), 1852–1872.

Griffin, R. A. (2012). I AM an angry Black woman: Black feminist autoethnography, voice, and resistance. *Women's Studies in Communication, 35*(2), 138–157.

Guzzetti, B. J., & Gamboa, M. (2004). Zines for social justice: Adolescent girls writing on their own. *Reading Research Quarterly, 39*(4), 408–436.

Hogan, M. J. (2020). Collaborative positive psychology: Solidarity, meaning, resilience, wellbeing, and virtue in a time of crisis. *International Review of Psychiatry, 32*(7–8), 698–712.

Holmes, M. (2004). Feeling beyond rules: Politicizing the sociology of emotion and anger in feminist politics. *European Journal of Social Theory, 7*(2), 209–227.

Hong, C. P. (2020). *Minor feelings: An Asian American reckoning*. One World.

Iftikar, J. S., & Museus, S. D. (2018). On the utility of Asian critical (AsianCrit) theory in the field of education. *International Journal of Qualitative Studies in Education, 31*(10), 935–949.

Jeong, E. (2019). *Koreangry #7*. https://koreangry.gumroad.com/l/QXgAQ

Jeong, E. (2020). *Koreangry #9*. https://koreangry.gumroad.com/l/koreangry9

Kay, J. B., & Banet-Weiser, S. (2019). Feminist anger and feminist respair. *Feminist Media Studies, 19*(4), 603–609.

Kim, S. J. (2011). Anger, temporality, and the politics of reading the woman warrior. In F. L. Aldama (Ed.), *Analyzing world fiction* (pp. 93–108). University of Texas Press.

Kwon, H. (2020). Emotion and critical pedagogy: Community art workshops for women at Midlands Shelter as critical emotional praxis. *Visual Arts Research, 46*(2), 68–84.

Lebron, C. J. (2017). *The making of Black Lives Matter: A brief history of an idea*. Oxford University Press.

Leng, K. (2020). Art, humor, and activism: The sardonic, sustaining feminism of the Guerrilla Girls, 1985–2000. *Journal of Women's History, 32*(4), 110–134.

Lorde, A. (1997). The uses of anger. *Women's Studies Quarterly, 25*(1/2), 278–285.

Mora, A. R. (2018). Reading a complex Latina stereotype: An analysis of modern family's Gloria Pritchett, intersectionality, and audiences. In A. A. Williams, R. Tsuria, L. Robinson, & A. Khilnani (Eds.), *Media and power in international contexts: Perspectives on agency and identity* (Vol. 16, pp. 133–151). Emerald Publishing Limited.

Orgad, S., & Gill, R. (2019). Safety valves for mediated female rage in the# MeToo era. *Feminist Media Studies, 19*(4), 596–603.

Phoenix, D. L. (2019). *The anger gap: How race shapes emotion in politics* (1st ed.). Cambridge University Press.

Piepmeier, A. (2009). *Girl zines: Making media, doing feminism*. New York University Press.
Rhee, J. (2013). The neoliberal racial project: The tiger mother and governmentality. *Educational Theory*, *63*(6), 561–580.
Stenberg, S. (2011). Teaching and (re)learning the rhetoric of emotion. *Pedagogy: Critical Approaches to Teaching Literature, Language, Composition, and Culture*, *11*(2), 349–369.
Stevenson, B. (2013). *The contested murder of Latasha Harlins: Justice, gender, and the origins of the LA Riots*. OUP USA.
Thompson, S. (2006). Anger and the struggle for justice. In S. Clarke, P. Hoggett, & S. Thompson (Eds.), *Emotion, politics and society* (pp. 123–144). Palgrave Macmillan UK.
Weida, C. L. (2013). Feminist zines:(Pre) occupations of gender, politics, and DIY in a digital age. *Journal of Social Theory in Art Education*, *33*(1), 67–85.
Zembylas, M. (2007). Mobilizing anger for social justice: The politicization of the emotions in education. *Teaching Education*, *18*(1), 15–28.

PART III

DE-CENTERING WHITE CURRICULAR CANONS

CHAPTER 13

WITNESSING CALLS TO ACTION

An Anti-Racist Education Through a Public Curriculum of the Arts

Addyson Frattura and Yotam Ronen
University of British Columbia

In the aftermath of the murder of George Floyd, Black activists and thinkers continue to call on white people to take on one's own learning in ourselves and in our communities. Such learning constitutes the commitment to fight against anti-Black racism. Inspired by this call and cognizant of academia's role in perpetuating racism, we created a participatory curriculum project that decenters learning and positions it in the hands of learners as both creators and students. We argue that making space for an arts-based learning that honors music, literature, and scholarship, invites learners to become active members in curricular creation and positions white people to enter meaningful conversations about racism and white supremacy that result in action. This project initiates a step toward the vital calls by Black thinkers and activists to take charge of our own learning and to fight alongside them in the struggle against white supremacy.

INTRODUCTION

In the aftermath of the murder of George Floyd at the hands of police officer Derek Chauvin on May 25, 2020, many voiced shock at the violence of Floyd's killing.

His death sparked a flurry of support for Black communities in the United States (US), and many white people sought to better understand the oppression of Black people. The desire translated, among other things, into record book sales about race, policing, and white supremacy (McEvoy, 2020). Yet, this sudden interest in Black lives was often superficial. White people reading about racism was seen as performative, as it didn't result in immediate action. "White people tend to take a slow route to meaningful activism, locked in familiar patterns, seemingly uninterested in really advancing progress" (Johnson, 2020). Such slow engagement often forces Black people to relive histories of racialized trauma and culminates with white people neglecting responsibility (Wilson, 2020).

Importantly, our schooling and education work to obscure understandings of racial oppression while promoting whiteness as the norm (West et al., 1995). This we must understand and confront in ourselves. What follows is an invitation to study oneself and society through an arts-based public curriculum, in response to calls to action against white supremacy, an institution that intimately and violently constructs experiences of race and domination of the white normative (Kombua'Ervin, 2006). We first position the call for action in its theoretical, social, and historical context. We then outline our curriculum project, discuss its framing through an arts-based curriculum, contend with peer review feedback, and finally discuss movements toward making this curriculum public.

THE CALL IN CONTEXT

Answering the call means acting in solidarity with Black communities. This requires many actions, from material support to partnership in revolutionary work. However, while acting in solidarity, white people should not put themselves at the center of liberatory movements, but should follow members of oppressed communities on what forms of allyship are needed (Kombua'Ervin, 2006). Whatever the action, it requires a leap of faith, and is fraught with mistakes, discomfort, and uncertainty (Oluo, 2018).

This call to action is not new. In his speech at Grosse Pointe High School, Martin Luther King Jr. claimed that contending with the issue of race requires recognition that the US is a racist country, and that cooperating with racism only leads to genocide (King Jr., 1968). James Baldwin (1963) asserted earlier that this recognition, which is at the heart of education, is dangerous because it demands the learner dispute the status quo and its assertion of the normative. To do otherwise would mean to live in myth. For Baldwin, myths are lies about our shared history and values that shape our actions and social understandings. Prominent myths in the US, for example, are that the white colonists were heroic and successful in "forming" the US, or that any person can prosper regardless of class, gender, skin color, etc. (Baldwin, 1963).

For bell hooks (1996), the way out of these myths begins by recognizing how we as white people benefit from white supremacy. White people are being asked to not live in myth, to unsettle ourselves, and to take responsibility for our learning. This ask requires the learner to understand this educative unsettling as a precursor—and at times a companion—to action, rather than performing superficial and temporary value signaling. Here, we intend to take a small, yet meaningful, step in this direction through engaging with art. In what follows, we illustrate an arts-based, public curriculum as one form of anti-racist education.

ART AS ANTI-RACIST EDUCATION

We suggest one way to take responsibility for one's anti-racist education is through immersing oneself in a public curriculum of the arts. To immerse is to embrace the maxim that learning never concludes and that one never arrives at absolute knowledge. Learning continues to expand as it nurtures one's understanding and capacity to act. In what follows, "our" signifies white people—the authors included—who have been asked for centuries to respond to calls for racial justice, and to abolish racist systems. Our proposed curriculum of the arts does not need to be formal. We already swim in the cultural curriculum of literature, music, and the visual and performing arts. To respond in this way is to pay critical attention to what surrounds us.

This is not a mere imbibing of artistic pursuits born from the realities of race in the US, nor is it the appropriation of art made by Black creators. This is not a possessive act, but a serious act of study and attention. A public, arts-based curriculum as an anti-racist education is an act of witnessing, where one becomes a stranger to something both known and unknown (Greene, 1973). We lean on the magnitude and possibility of artistic creations and imaginations. Our learning in this way cannot be passive, for that would not be a true education. It is "your being [that] has to be changed," Bettina Love declares of abolitionist teaching. Such an education "is a push for everybody's humanity" (Love et al., 2020). In the transformation of one's being, culture is the curriculum and racist systems are abolished, not reformed. We note art as what often provokes social consciousness, and follow Toni Morrison and Angela Davis's reasoning for positioning art as a critical and abundant place to begin. An arts-based public curriculum shapes our social consciousness of race and self.

Toni Morrison's work shapes the social consciousness and responds to the construction of race through literature. Morrison was often asked when she would write something *not* about race, meaning something about white people, knowing well that white authors would never be asked this question. To ask this question is to forget that you too are "raced" (Morrison, 1998). And within that question is the belief that "there's the center, which is white, and then there are these regional Blacks or Asians, or any sort of marginal people. That question can only be asked from the center." Morrison positions a call of her own: "I'm gonna stay out here on the margin, and let the center look for me" (Morrison, 1993).

As we go looking for Morrison, we recall that she never intended to write for the white gaze. "It does not have to do with who reads the books," Morrison clarifies, "but my sovereignty and my authority as a racialized person had to be struck immediately with the very first book" (Morrison, 1998). Morrison's sovereignty is so crucial, as white writers often create oppressive images of Black people which feed a racist social consciousness. These constructed images generate severe consequences for the "literary imagination" and perhaps also for the social imagination of what is possible and who is valued as human (Morrison, 1992, p. x).

Morrison's writing required her to "learn...ways to free up the language from its sometimes sinister, frequently lazy, almost always predictable employment of racially informed and determined chains" (Morrison, 1992, p. xi). Blackness is often forced to linger near the literary margins, while the canon of American literature safeguards the white male view. The white male is shaped in his contrast from "the racial other" (Morrison, 1992, p. 46). Through constructed and sinister difference, his identity is born. James Baldwin, for example, writes about the harmful ramifications of representations of Black people in literature and film (Baldwin, 1998). Blackness is "central to any understanding of our national literature" and should not be marginalized (Morrison, 1992, p. 5). While literature often generates such determinative images, it also prompts us to enter unfamiliar realms. This is the imaginative power of "becoming" through reading and thinking (Morrison, 1992, p. 4).

Literature is a public curriculum that shapes our social consciousness. Our social and "cultural identities" are shaped by our literature, which fashions the intentional creation of difference. White people benefit from the "consolidating [of] identity along [these] culturally valuable lines of interest" (Morrison, 1992, p. 39). An anti-racist education is not just reading. It is what you read, how you read, who you read with, and how it influences the cultivation of your thinking and being. Reading Morrison as white readers, we confront a world uninterpreted for us, in which we are strangers. In line with Morrison, this is a necessary education for the white social consciousness.

The shaping of social consciousness often happens through literature because visual and linguistic devices bleed into "the social and political nature of received knowledge" (Morrison, 1992, p. 49). The construction of race through literature positions race as a "metaphorical" reference to power, class, as well as "social decay and economic division." This severely imperils the nation, more than biological "race" ever has (Morrison, 1992, p. 63). Artists respond by "clarifying, explicating, valorizing, translating, transforming, [and] criticizing" (Morrison, 1992, p. 49). However, this is often contradictory, as many nineteenth century writers were shaped by competing commitments to both a free republic and the institution of slavery. Importantly, we receive a cultural education through literature, whether we know it or not, and whether we like it or not. The question is what we do with it.

Furthermore, it is not only literature that educates us. Music informs our understandings of self and other. Angela Davis (1999) writes of the Blues legacy through Gertrude "Ma" Rainey, Bessie Smith, and Billie Holiday, whose music shaped American culture. Their recorded performances expose legacies of "feminist consciousness in working-class black [sic] communities" which were previously unrecognized. While Black women were the first to record the Blues, they were exploited and marginalized within the musical tradition (Davis, 1999). The origin of the Blues through these women is significant insofar as they each "left behind [...] hints of feminist attitudes [that] emerge from their music through fissures of patriarchal discourse" (p. xi). They made the Blues provocative and educative; they initiated "possibilities of sustaining emergent feminist consciousness" as they boldly navigated contradictions of subservience, sovereignty, and defiance (Davis, 1999, p. xv).

One particular Blues song has reverberated throughout our history and present realities. "Strange Fruit" by Billie Holiday is a song that "evoked the horrors of lynching at a time when black [sic] people were still passionately calling for allies in the campaign to eradicate this murderous and terroristic manifestation of racism" (Davis, 1999, p. 183). Originally published as a poem by Abel Meerpool in 1937, a white Jewish teacher, Holiday sings the opening lines: "Southern trees bear a strange fruit / Blood on the leaves and blood at the root / Black bodies swingin' in the Southern breeze / Strange fruit hangin' from the poplar trees." The song divulged from "sociohistorical [sic] circumstances," similarly to how Morrison described artists' response. The conditions from which the song was crafted offered a strong base for the public acceptance of "an impassioned plea for racial justice" (Davis, 1999, p. 189) and expanded through the Harlem Renaissance of the 1920s and the NAACP's antilynching campaigns of the 1930s. This song "almost singlehandedly [sic] changed the politics of American popular culture and put the elements of protest and resistance back at the center of contemporary black musical culture" (Davis, 1999, p. 184).

"Strange Fruit" attained something beyond "permanent preservation" as millions of people listened to Holiday sing the "haunting antilynching appeal." Witnessing and listening to this song later prompted "people to discover within themselves a previously unawakened calling to political activism." The anti-lynching poem turned song continues to be one of the most significant instances of "the intersection of music and social consciousness" (Davis, 1999, p. 195-196). As we write this, "Strange Fruit" continues to reverberate, as do songs like Childish Gambino's "This is America" and LG Team Genius' "YBM," circulating after more police killings: "Black man dead, white cop is alive... cell phones caught it but the body cam died" (LG Team Genius, 2021).

AN ARTS-BASED CURRICULUM PROJECT

Our task is to respond to Davis' call of awakening to political activism through music, to forget the white normative center, and go look for Morrison where she stands. We must move away from professing a "righteous indignation of the masses" after racialized harm. Such a response, James Haywood Rolling Jr. (2020) writes, seldom leads to justice. He continues that both Black lives matter and art matters "toward the achievement of social justice...the value of each life and every creative act indispensably enriches us all" (p. 8). In responding to the calls to be actively anti-racist, to protect Black lives, and to fight institutional racism, we propose one entry point, inspired by the cultural curriculum and social consciousness provoked by art. We offer a study route for ourselves and others to contend with the harmful and oppressive realities of anti-Black racism that our worldview and experiences have been created from and through. It is important to note that we, the authors, are both non-racialized and white PhD students in the Faculty of Education on the traditional, ancestral, and unceded territory of the xʷməθkʷəẏəm (Musqueam), Skwxwú7mesh (Squamish), and the Səlílwətaʔ/Selilwitulh (Tsleil-Waututh) First Nations, in so-called Vancouver, BC. We are guided by our varying backgrounds, identities, and experiences as a queer woman from the rural Midwestern US and a Jewish man from Israel.

The project began from questioning the inadequacy of responses to anti-Black racism through the performative allyship of educational institutions. We began by organizing a reading group, which meets regularly to read, study, and discuss ways toward action. Yet, engaging with critiques shared earlier, we realized that a reading group is not enough. As graduate students in education, we felt we should take action through our capacities in pedagogy and curriculum. We designed a curriculum project that begins within the public discourse of music, art, and literature as an anchor point. It provides a guided study route to initiate, nourish, and support an educated and self-reflective activism.

While the initial route is not comprehensive, it is a useful step toward transformative learning for those of us who are not Black in North America. Our aim is not to teach as if we have already arrived. Rather, this project serves as a platform for continued learning in community and encourages the creation of additional study routes with similar ethical convictions. Rather than a stand-alone reading list, we offer a suggested study route, which prompts the learner to listen, read, think, question, write, dialogue, engage, and act. This guided form of self-study ends in a non-ending, as the learner is supported in expanding their study and returning to the materials and questions from which they began.

The route and suggested texts bloom from our initial studying of the song "This is America" by Childish Gambino and Gambino's film, *Guava Island* where "America is a concept" (Murai, 2019). Based on the song's context and themes, we studied it as a site of learning through two themes: *voice* and *capital*. The reader can see an example of what this might look like in Figure 13.1. From there we developed questions, study materials, and a guided study route that offers the learner two options. Option One: Dig in and Read. Option Two: Guided Digging. The first option includes a narrated bibliography with questions. The second option offers a supported framework for self-learning through the readings and themes. While this is a curriculum project, anti-racist education is not about content and curriculum alone. It ultimately concerns the learner, whose being is provoked and transformed.

Witnessing Calls to Action • 123

"This is America"
Childish Gambino
(Donald Glover)

The tone of and music of the intro feels light, simply almost celebratory, until it radically shifts in tone when the 1st verse hits.

For me, this verse reads like a comment on the uses and abuses of black culture, where blackness, that is temporarily coopted as a critique of capitalism and meekness is used to benefit capitalist ventures, and further entrench racist stereotypes.

Who is the "we"?

what is meant by "party" and what is meant by "free"? And what kind of price do you pay to "party for free"? I am curious about this phrase.

Me too. Why is this "this"? Is that America? The US? Who is it?

curious of other usages of this phrase in history and the significance and meaning of Gambino's uptake here. The one that always comes to mind for me is David Bowie's "This is not America" recorded with Pat Metheny.

Yeah, yeah, yeah, yeah, yeah → *who or what is the subject here?*
Yeah, yeah, yeah, go, go away
Yeah, yeah, yeah, yeah, yeah
Yeah, yeah, yeah, go, go away
Yeah, yeah, yeah, yeah, yeah
Yeah, yeah, yeah, yeah, yeah
Yeah, yeah, yeah, yeah, yeah
Yeah, yeah, yeah, go, go away
We just wanna party
Party just for you → *who is the "you"?*
We just want the money → *reminds me of "us" and "them" phrasing in US political debate*
Money just for you
I know you wanna party (yeah)
Party just for free → *is this the same "you"?*
Girl, you got me dancin' (girl, you got me dancin')
Dance and shake the frame
We just wanna party (yeah)
Party just for you (yeah)
We just want the money (yeah) → *It would be interesting to look at works that look at dance as forms of protest, especially with the clip for this song in mind.*
Money just for you (ooh)
I know you wanna party (yeah)
Party just for free (yeah)
Girl, you got me dancin' (girl, you got me dancin')
Dance and shake the frame (ooh)
This is America → *I wonder about Gambino's intention behind this song.*
Don't catch you slippin' now
Don't catch you slippin' now
Look what I'm whippin' now
This is America (woo)
Don't catch you slippin' now
Don't catch you slippin' now
Look what I'm whippin' now
This is America (skrrt, skrrt, woo) → *What is the significance of these utterances, which are not words at all, but to form an important part of the song?*
Don't catch you slippin' now (ayy)
Look at how I'm livin' now
Police be trippin' now (woo)
Yeah, this is America (woo, ayy)
Guns in my area (word, my area)
I got the strap (ayy, ayy) → *This is a technique called "doubling," and is used for emphasis. Why did he decide to emphasize this over other words? Why "area" and not "Guns"?*
I gotta carry 'em

3

FIGURE 13.1.

As we move forward, we intend to thicken this curriculum alongside key figures who cultivated substantial frameworks from which our work emerges. We owe gratitude to Keisha N. Blain and Ibram X. Kendi's (2017) commitment to challenging a "post-scholar America" through public scholarship, public syllabi, and shifting values wherein academic work is "deeply scholarly," and "fully accessible" (para. 15). They have shown how this can be done through their work as editors of the blog Black Perspectives, as well as their public curriculum and anti-racist education contributions (Kendi, 2016; Kendi, 2019; Kendi & Blain, 2021).

Many scholars, educators, and artists inform our work, such as Verna St. Denis' (2007) work on anti-racist education and pedagogy, bell hooks' (1994, 1996, 2003) dreaming and writing on education, freedom, and community teaching, and Marina Ortega and Linda Martín Alcoff's (2009) scholarship on constructions of race and nation. We build from Bettina Love's (2019) development of abolitionist teaching and from other scholars such as Jorge Lucero (2010), Michelle Kraft and Karen Keifer-Boyd (2013), Albert Stabler (2018), and Adetty de Miles Perez (2019).

WHERE WE ARE AND WHERE WE ARE HEADED

Here we suggest an arts-based public curriculum as an anti-racist education. However, the relationship crafted between race and art is not new. Cherríe Moraga, Gloria Anzaldúa, and AnaLouise Keating write of the intersections of identity, oppression, and liberation of women of color through art (Moraga & Anzaldúa 2015; Anzaldúa & Keating 2002). Aruna D'Souza offers us an example of the complicated nexus of the art world and institutional racism (D'Souza, 2018). Mariana Ortega helps us to deepen our understanding of Morrison and Davis' legacies through the concept of "aesthetic unsettlement" which can interrupt "pervasive, settled modes of knowledge and ignorance regarding race" (Ortega, 2019, p.126).

This curriculum project takes seriously the call for non-racialized people to educate ourselves and our communities through a public, arts-based curriculum that prioritizes open-ended curricular engagements. To do so, we engaged community reviewers, many of whom appreciated the self-reflective model, the unifying text of the song, and the listening companions of music and podcasts. Some celebrated the two study routes as helpful because an extensive reading list can be overwhelming, while the guided digging offers deeper engagement. One reviewer suggested an introduction to identity, power, and intersectionality for learners that are new to anti-racist work, as well as discussing our motivations for selecting the song "This is America." Others prompted the inclusion of more visual artists to further trouble the notion of a "text," and some noted our annotations of the song as primary text as specific to our situated experiences, prompting us to consider the dispositions of learners who will have different questions.

Our intention now is two-fold; first, we intend to make our pilot project available for wide distribution by uploading it to an online repository. Second, we plan to create a platform where others can create their own curricular anchors (visual art pieces, poetry, film, music, or any other anchor around which both racialized oppression and joyful futures can be explored). By creating a space of learning that is collaborative, interactive, and that utilizes various art forms, we hope to inspire a will for action in learners, which goes beyond the superficial engagements that we are rightfully accused of. It is our intention that learners become partners in anti-racist education through a public, arts-based curriculum that shifts our understandings of self and social consciousness. We do not claim that a public, arts-based curriculum is more powerful than direct action. Nor do we profess that it is more substantial than institutionalized educational programs that study racial oppression. What we advocate for is a serious interrogation of the self and social consciousness, and we suggest that one avenue to do this is through the evocative power of a public curriculum of the arts.

REFERENCES

Anzaldúa, G., & Keating, A. (2002). *This bridge we call home: Radical visions for transformation.* Routledge. https://doi.org/10.4324/9780203952962

Baldwin, J. (1963). *A talk to teachers.* Zinn Education Project. https://www.zinnedproject.org/materials/baldwin-talk-to-teachers/

Baldwin, J. (1998). *Collected essays* (T. Morrison, Ed.). Library of America.

Blain, K., & Kendi, I. X. (2017). How to avoid a post-scholar America. *Chronicle of Higher Education, 63*(39), 1-1. https://www.chronicle.com/article/how-to-avoid-a-post-scholar-america/

Davis, A. (1999). *Blues legacies and black feminism: Gertrude "Ma" Rainey, Bessie Smith, and Billi eHoliday.* Vintage Books.

D'Souza, A. (2018). Park Bright and Pastiche Lumumba, illustrators. *Whitewalling: Art, race, & protest in 3 acts.* Badlands Unlimited.

Greene, M. (1973). *Teacher as stranger: Educational philosophy for the modern age.* Wadsworth Publishing Company.

Haywood Rolling, J. Jr. (2020). Making Black Lives Matter: Toward an anti-racist artmaking and teaching agenda-Part 1. *Art Education, 73*(5), 8–9. https://doi.org/10.1080/00043125.2020.1796200

hooks, b. (1994). *Teaching to transgress: Education as the practice of freedom.* Routledge. https://doi.org/10.4324/9780203700280.

hooks, b. (1996). *Killing rage: Ending racism.* Holt.

hooks, b. (2003). *Teaching community: A pedagogy of hope.* Routledge. https://doi.org/10.4324/9780203957769

Johnson, T. (2020). When black people are in pain, white people just join book clubs. *The Washington Post.* https://www.washingtonpost.com/outlook/white-antiracist-allyship-book-clubs/2020/06/11/9edcc766-abf5-11ea-94d2-d7bc43b26bf9_story.html

Kendi, I. (2016). *Stamped from the beginning: The definitive history of racist ideas in America.* Bold Type Books.

Kendi, I. (2019). *How to be an antiracist.* One World.

Kendi, I., & Blain, K. (Eds.). (2021). *Four hundred souls: A community history of African America, 1619–2019.* One World.

King Jr., Rev. M. L. (1968, 03). *The Other America—Speech at the Grosse Pointe High School.* Grosse Pointe Historical Society. https://www.gphistorical.org/mlk/mlk-speech/

Komboa'Ervin, L. (2016). Anarchism and the Black Revolution. In *Black anarchism—A reader by the Black Rose Anarchist Federation* (pp. 10–71). Black Rose Anarchist Federation. https://www.blackrosefed.org/wp-content/uploads/2016/02/Black-Anarchism-A-Reader-4.pdf

Kraft, M., & Keifer-Boyd, K. (2013). *Including difference: A communitarian approach to art education in the least restrictive environment.* National Art Education Association.

LG (Team Genius). (2021). *Song.* YBM. https://www.youtube.com/watch?v=iZWF2ydR1bs&ab_channel=LGTeamGenius.

Love, B. (2019). *We want to do more than survive: Abolitionist teaching and the pursuit of educational freedom.* Beacon Press.

Love, B., Muhammad, G., Simmons, D., & Brian Jones (2020, June 23). *Abolitionist teaching and the future of our schools* [Webinar]. Haymarket Books. https://www.youtube.com/watch?v=uJZ3RPJ2rNc&ab_channel=HaymarketBooks

Lucero, J. R. (2010). *Teach yourself: Student as contemporary practitioner.* Unpublished workshop script & scavenger hunt directives, 2010–14. https://www.academia.edu/44471705/TEACH_YOURSELF_STUDENT_AS_CONTEMPORARY_PRACTITIONER

McEvoy, J. (2020). *Sales of 'white fragility'—And other anti-racism books—Jumped over 2000% after protests began.* Forbes. https://www.forbes.com/sites/jemimamcevoy/2020/07/22/sales-of-white-fragility-and-other-anti-racism-books-jumped-over-2000-after-protests-began/

Meerpool, A. (1937). Strange fruit [Poem]. In *The strange story of the man behind 'strange fruit.'* NPR. https://www.npr.org/2012/09/05/158933012/the-strange-story-of-the-man-behind-strange-fruit.

Moraga, C., & Anzaldúa, G. (2015). *This bridge called my back: Writings by radical women of color.* (SUNY) Press.

Morrison, T. (1992) *Playing in the dark.* Vintage Books.

Morrison, T. (1993). Interview by Elissa Schappel and Claudia Brodsky Lacour, "The Art of Fiction No. 134" *Paris Review,* https://www.theparisreview.org/interviews/1888/the-art-of-fiction-no-134-toni-morrison

Morrison, T. (1998). *Interview with Charlie Rose.* https://charlierose.com/videos/17664

Murai, H. (Director). (2019). *Guava Island.* [Film]. Amazon Studios.

Oluo, I. (2018). *So you want to talk about race* (1st ed.). Seal Press.

Ortega, M. (2019). Bodies of color, bodies of sorrow: On resistant sorrow, aesthetic unsettlement, and becoming-with. *Critical Philosophy of Race, 7*(1), 124–143.

Ortega, M., & Alcoff, L. M. (Eds.). (2009). *Constructing the nation: A race and nationalism reader.* SUNY Press.

Pérez Miles, A. (2019). Unbound philosophies & histories: Epistemic disobedience in contemporary Latin American art. In J. Baldacchino (Ed.), *The international encyclopedia of art and design education Histories and philosophies of art & design education* (vol. 1). Wiley-Blackwell and the National Society of Art and Design Education (NSEAD).

Stabler, A. (2018). The white art teacher's burden: aesthetics, pedagogy, and political self-awareness. *Visual Arts Research, 44*(2), 87.

St. Denis, V. (2007). Aboriginal education and anti-racist education: Building alliances across cultural and racial identity. *Journal of Education 30,*(4), 1068–1092.

West, C., Crenshaw, K., Gotanda, N., Peller, G., & Thomas, K. (1995). *Critical race theory: The key writings that formed the movement.* The New Press.

Wilson, B. L. (2020). Perspective | I'm your black friend, but I won't educate you about racism. That's on you. *Washington Post.* https://www.washingtonpost.com/outlook/2020/06/08/black-friends-educate-racism/

CHAPTER 14

BUILDING BETTER CURRICULUM THROUGH BLACK HAIR

Linda Hoeptner Poling
Kent State University

Juliann Dorff
Kent State University

This chapter outlines our journey as two White professors who created an art curriculum based on the exhibition TEXTURES: The History and Art of Black Hair (Ellington & Underwood, 2020) that took place at our predominately White institution. We investigate the intersection of our Whiteness within critical race and critical feminist race theories, which anchored every step. Our process of moving through the work, learning to merge from cultural competence to cultural humility, enabled us to be successful. We describe both our process and the curriculum.

Keywords: Critical Race Theory; Critical Feminist Race Theory; Texturism; Cultural Humility

We are two White women art educators on a journey to do their part to disrupt and re-write hegemonic White narratives that pervade art education curricula. In this chapter, we unpack and deconstruct the process of creating

Educator Resources that accompany the exhibit TEXTURES: The History and Art of Black Hair (Ellington & Underwood, 2020) that took place at Kent State University 2021-2022. We describe how we bridge to both a critical race theory consciousness and to a critical feminist race theory consciousness that anchored our work; and the first bridges we took, merging from cultural competence to cultural humility, enabling us to do the work authentically. A diversity audit was the final step to ensure Black experiences were centered in the curriculum, and we shared when our Whiteness got in the way of authenticity. We provide an overview of TEXTURES as an exemplar of *testimonio*.

As social justice art educators, we acknowledge this work must be done within a lens of awareness of our own social positionings and identities (Acevedo et al., 2015). In this spirit, we provide our positionality for the reader. As faculty members at Kent State University, a predominantly White institution, we have collaborated as colleagues since our first meeting more than twenty years ago. Linda Hoeptner Poling is in her mid-50s and is mother to two grown children. She has taught art in diverse K–12 settings. Juliann Dorff, in her early 70s, also with two grown children, taught K–8 art in a parochial school.

BRIDGING TO A CRT AND CRITICAL FEMINIST RACE THEORY CONSCIOUSNESS

Critical race theory (CRT), first conceptualized by legal scholars in the 1970s following advancements, then the stalling of, the civil rights era of the 1960s, is used to understand how inequities persist in all facets of the educational milieu. Within both a personal and an activist framework, CRT is applied to transform educational practice and conditions for the better (Delgado & Stefancic, 2001). Renowned educational scholars, Gloria Ladson-Billings and William Tate, introduced CRT at the 1995 AERA conference and that same year published a seminal paper on the topic, "Toward a critical race theory of education." In that work, Ladson-Billings and Tate provided three distinct lenses for understanding the applications of CRT in education, including the ubiquity of race as a factor in inequity in the U.S.; the basis of property rights in the U.S.; and the intersection of race and property as factors in understanding educational inequities (Ladson-Billings & Tate, 1995). Ladson-Billings (2005) urges anyone driven to address persistent racial inequities in U.S. schools to be inspired by CRT.

Our work in part attends to a critical feminist race theory orientation that calls for organizational accountability from critical examination of hegemonic structures and practices that privilege White patriarchal colonialism and the intersections between race, gender, class, and other social identifiers within that orientation (Cisneros, 2021; Verjee, 2012). We rely on the framework of CRT to aid in our understanding of inequities and racial oppression and how to eradicate those same racial inequities and racial oppression. We additionally apply the lens of gender (Collins, et al., 2021; Crenshaw, 1989; Deliu & Ilea, 2018) as it intersects with those same categories, and whenever plausible and appropriate, applied a critical feminist race theoretical positionality to our TEXTURES curriculum work, as will later be discussed in this paper.

Acuff (2019) reflects on this kind of work, situating it within a milieu that overlaps and intersects with the field of art education, which is a predominantly White site":..social justice art education, critical multicultural art education, culturally relevant and/or responsive art education, socially engaged art education, and critical race art education generally center the narratives of people of color because oftentimes their knowledge, lived experiences and contributions are absent and/or ignored in mainstream art education discourse, research and classrooms" (p. 8). From the onset, we acknowledged the importance of centering the voices and lived experiences of Black people in our TEXTURES curriculum. We next describe the steps needed to enable us to do the work meaningfully as two White women with limited experiences describing our years-long process of building cultural humility.

BRIDGING FROM CULTURAL COMPETENCE TO CULTURAL HUMILITY

Debates over critiques of cultural competence versus cultural humility have received wide critical analysis. While both are problematic, there are sound arguments for aligning with the less tokenistic notion of the anti-oppressive diversity practice of cultural humility (Danso, 2018). Cultural competence emerged from social work within a multicultural context and can be defined as "the process by which individuals and systems respond respectfully and effectively to people of all cultures, languages, classes, races, ethnic backgrounds, religions, spiritual traditions, immigration status, and other diversity factors in a manner that recognizes, affirms, values, and preserves their dignity" (Danso, 2018, pp. 413-414). Calls to challenge one's own assumptions, Whiteness, Eurocentricity, and values came out of this construct, and cultural competence efforts were integrated within social justice work. Interrogating its limitations, including failing to acknowledge racial oppression, critics called out the framework: "The wide diversities and differences that exist within cultures coupled with the fluidity of culture itself limit anyone's ability to be competent at another culture" (Danso, 2018, p. 416).

Cultural humility followed the cultural competence lens and emerged in the medical field within a framework of delivering culturally appropriate medical care. Self-critique and self-reflection are key markers of cultural humility, as is redressing power imbalances, with expected outcomes that disrupt and re-shape oppressive institutional forces for positive community outcomes. Practicing cultural humility encourages one "to learn from the clients [in our case learners] and communities they work with about both their past and current experiences, as well as learn from the perspectives and interpretations that other people give to their personal experiences" (Danso, 2018, p. 423). Intrapersonal awareness to one's own limitations to understanding cultures different than one's own, and interpersonal awareness marked by an openness to and respect for increased understanding, are hallmarks of cultural humility.

DEPARTING FROM CULTURAL COMPETENCE

The premise of multicultural education was very much in both our consciousnesses and understood as integrated into our practices for decades as we prepared future art educators to be multicultural art educators. Sonia Nieto's (1992) notion of pluralism, as connected to multicultural education, resonated with us: "Multicultural education is a process of comprehensive school reform and basic education for all students. This process challenges and rejects racism and other forms of discrimination in schools and society and accepts and affirms the pluralism" (p. 208). Beyond this, we also actively work to center discourse around social justice art education and work to include all voices in all aspects of art pedagogy; being each other's sounding boards for this work is part of our daily practice. We briefly next describe those early works that contributed to our early awareness.

Lucy Lippard's *Mixed Blessings* (2000) anchored our love of contemporary Black, Indigenous, and People of Color (BIPOC) artists. We were fueled by Susan Cahan and Zoya Kocur's *Contemporary Art and Multicultural Education* (1996) and the follow-up *Rethinking Contemporary Art and Multicultural Education* by New Museum (2011) and enthusiastically (still) require our pre-service students to use a majority of contemporary artists in their curriculum planning to increase awareness and acceptance of the here-and-now realities of experiences *their* students face.

Critical ethnographies such as *Ain't No Makin' It: Aspirations & Attainment in a Low-Income Neighborhood* (MacLeod, 1995), *The Dreamkeepers: Successful Teachers of African American Teachers* (Ladson-Billings, 1994), and *Touching Eternity: The Enduring Outcomes of Teaching* (Barone, 2001) heightened our lenses of critical understanding of the complexities of multiculturalism within educational spaces, during a time we both were teaching in K–12. Critical theorist Paulo Freire (1992) and feminist critical theorist bell hooks (1984, 1994) also shaped our thinking, leading, and guiding our early consciousness and practices in intersectional social justice art education intersecting with multicultural art education.

Additionally, Joel Spring's *Deculturalization and the Struggle for Equality: A Brief History of the Education of Dominated Cultures in the United States* (2nd Ed.) (1997) deeply impacted us both, spotlighting how mainstream educational landscapes systemically contribute to the erasure of BIPOC peoples' identities and cultural traditions and replacing them with the dominant group's own language and culture.

These early influences helped create a dynamic nexus from which we created a curriculum at our institution to prepare our pre-service teachers and the foundation for the Educator Resources. They helped build a critical cultural competence in us both, which created conditions ripe to begin building cultural humility.

While serving on the Kent State University Anti-Racism Task Force in 2021, Linda was asked by a Black male colleague what she was personally doing to stop anti-Black racism at the University. His question was fair, and one that must be answered, without defensiveness and with honesty. I shared with him the number of presentations that Juli and I have given, including, at the risk of sounding imperious, on BIPOC contemporary artists and a number of DEI + Belonging town halls, and service related to anti-racism. Not knowing if the answer satisfied him, I was sure the question mattered more than the answer. Showing up in this way, in part, contributes to building cultural humility that prepares White teachers to write curricula in culturally humble ways, as we have done.

Building Cultural Humility

Juli and I deliberately moved through self-analysis both individually and together, to engage humbly in cross- and inter-cultural understanding of the works and artists in the TEXTURES exhibition as we constructed our curriculum, as well as our relationship to the exhibition on a campus that is a predominantly White institution. Co-curators Tameka Ellington and Joseph Underwood note their awareness of having the TEXTURES exhibition on a predominantly White campus with a predominantly White viewership, stating, "this is what is important—so more can have an idea about Black joy and Black beauty." It is hard *not* to center the voices of the large majority of Black artists in the TEXTURES exhibition. We argue, however, that White art educators unconsciously reframe their lens of curriculum-writing to align with their Whiteness and default to Whiteness without a conscious effort to do otherwise, even when the artists that are represented are not White, in a tokenistic manner, if they are not prepared otherwise, as has been well documented (García, 2022). Instead, "Entering into uncomfortable conversations provide a way to disrupt the White ownership of art and education and reframe art education using *othered* experiences and perspectives" (García, 2022, p. xx) when it comes to re-envisioning art curriculum and is sorely needed.

We agree with Christine Sleeter (2016) that challenging and dismantling Whiteness in higher education is difficult and emotional work that does not become easier with time. She challenges White educators to see and come to terms with their privilege as such, to practice non-defensive and empathetic listening to the perspectives of people of color within a framework of allyship and openness to being questioned about their beliefs, especially when it comes to addressing issues of racism and their own racialized privileges. Juli and I learned to navigate how each of us in our Whiteness was personally perpetuating racialized inequities in our program, and more importantly, how we would support one another in ending those practices. We can be open and honest with each other because we have loved each other deeply as friends for so long. We feel safe in doing so. As we learn and grow in our cultural humility, we share our findings with one another and hold each other accountable. There is an unspoken expectation that our growth is synergistically dependent.

We did not put the failures of our Whiteness front and center in our consciousness, out loud, in our pre-service practices at first. Kim Cosier (2019), Sunny Spillane (2015), and Jeffrey Broome (2018) are role models who do, providing personal narratives of their work with pre-service art educators, and Deborah Filbin (2021) with her K–12 students, additionally intersecting with a feminist pedagogy perspective. We must (painfully) admit that due to our commitment to social justice art education, we were not confronting the reality of the benefits of being White in a predominantly White field. By practicing and teaching a socially transformative curriculum and pedagogy, we thought we were doing diversity, equity, and inclusion due diligence at our institution and in our field. We can now confront what it means to be White in a very White field because of the purposeful allyship work we conducted over time. In the past, work was done adjacent *to*, but not in allyship *with* our BIPOC institution community; we realized this difference through purposeful engagement in professional experience and allyship work. For example, our university provided release time for faculty to build leadership skills in creating a more inclusive environment. Linda worked through this program, and other initiatives, knowing fully that releasing statements in solidarity with our BIPOC colleagues without accompanying action is the worst kind of allyship. We got to work to become better, upstander allies; by serving on anti-racism task forces, participating in inclusive learning communities, holding town halls; serving on search committees to recruit diverse staff; and activating a pedagogy of empathetic listening to our BIPOC students and colleagues. We respectfully acknowledge our role in centering the voices of our BIPOC students and colleagues and embrace ally and upstander work at all opportunities.

Marit Dewhurst's (2019) work resonated with us deeply. Dewhurst unpacked, deconstructed, and racialized the concept of "nice" in higher art education. Juli and I both grapple with that word *nice* all the time. We both proudly admit to being supportive, assertive, and *nice* professors (what could possibly be problematic with *nice*?). Dewhurst turned "nice" on its head, saying, "I've listened as colleagues have shared how the code of composed niceness has often turned a cold shoulder to their perspectives and their very existence. And I've started to see it in glimmers myself—how the very niceness I've always embraced might actually be harming people" (pp. 2-3).

How many times have Juli and I failed our non-White colleagues through White-niceness? We were painfully aware that we were working with people harmed by racism; Tameka, a Black woman; Christina, a Black woman; and Joseph, an Asian American man. Dewhurst (2019) brought some concrete perspective to our pain that we struggled to articulate within the context of doing this curriculum work, which we hope contributes to anti-racism work: "People who are identified as white are harmed by limitations of their own capacity to be humane—perhaps a more psychic or spiritual violence" (p. 6).

We had tacit awareness of our racialized differences in meetings with Tameka, Joseph, and Christina (Christina Timmons, our graduate student and co-writer of the Educator Resources, and Curatorial Assistant of the TEXTURES exhibition); even having awareness that our hair was long, and straight, on the spectrum of "texturism" that is interrogated and deconstructed in this exhibition examining Black African experience past and present. We knew that all aspects of this work required not niceness but genuine and sincere humility and sensitivity on the front side. More so, we applied *critical* and self-reflective sensitivity, within a framework of critical race theory and critical feminist race theory. We listened to the artworks, the critical feminist race theory orientation, the co-curators of the exhibition, and each other when constructing the Educator Resources. We subsequently requested a diversity audit for each lesson.

DIVERSITY AUDIT OF THE EDUCATOR RESOURCES

Co-curators Tameka and Joseph had enough faith in us to write the Educator Resources. Tameka said in an interview:

> I have to say that when I found out that you and Juli wanted to do this project I was overjoyed, especially the relationship that I've had with you over the years and the work that we've done with DEI and University Diversity Action Council. So when you guys told me that you wanted to do it, I was like, yes, absolutely, I wouldn't have wanted it to be anybody else, you know, but you guys. And the fact that you thought enough of me, thought enough of Black culture, to even ask me to do that, meant a lot to me because oftentimes, unfortunately White people will tell Black stories without even asking Black people. You know, and so it meant a lot for me that, but I didn't expect anything else from you all. That's just how you and Juli roll. (personal communication, February 8, 2022)

Tameka generously agreed to conduct a diversity audit of our lessons to check for instances of inappropriate Whiteness in places where it should have been Black; we centered our experiences where others' life frameworks should have taken center stage. Hair anchored us; Tameka made sure our White hair did not stop us at our roots. The diversity audit gave an authentic voice to our lessons. We humbly shared our drafts, awaiting Tameka's feedback, admittedly nervous. We are trained to defend ourselves and our ideas as scholars, but to be *defensive* is different. Juli and I knew intuitively that to truly practice cultural humility, deep listening without being defensive had to become our modus operandi.

Words that contain Black cultural power and authenticity replaced White ones. In reflective prompts, Tameka reminded us to be as inclusive as possible. For example, in the I Resist/I Celebrate lesson, in discussing the work of Keturah Ariel's *Internal Battle*, Tameka crossed out "How can those without natural Black hair have a better understanding of this struggle and show support for this struggle (*which centers the experience of White learners*)? She inserted: "Why is it important to listen to yourself when making decisions? What can society do to help make the decision-making process easier? What can society do to help Keturah be able to celebrate her hair instead of being in 'battle' with it?" This re-centering of the focus decentered the White-centric emphasis of the original prompt Linda first wrote. In the same lesson, Tameka was also mindful of diverse representation, sure to include "Muslim, maybe favorite head covering/hijab" for a list of inclusive hair props to celebrate.

Additionally, in I Resist/I Celebrate, Nakeya Brown's *Hair Portrait #3* is the focus of a discussion, showing the artist gazing at the viewer as we question whether she is consuming or vomiting the hairpiece, which has a smooth texture, juxtaposed with the texture of the natural hair on her head. Tameka added to the prompt (in italics): Her direct gaze and eye contact with us, the viewer, challenges us to reconsider how societal standards are being forced down her throat; *and the throats of all Black people*; and to instead believe that Black hair is indeed beautiful hair. Here we see evidence of how Tameka found entry moments resonant with critical race theory to remind art educators and all who read the Educator Resources that inequities persist for Black people in no uncertain terms.

When the first draft of Juli's lesson was titled, I Am Unapologetically Me!, Tameka crossed out "Me," and wrote in "Black," again focusing our attention on the purpose of the Educator Resources: to center the experiences of Black people—*not* White people. Tameka patiently built our cultural humility throughout the process, and for this, we are better social justice art educators. The resulting I Am Unapologetically Black! lesson rightfully centers on Black people's experiences with the radical change of this one word.

Juli and I were particularly grateful to be given the opportunity to write a curriculum that honored aspects of critical feminist race theory (Childers-McKee & Hytten, 2017) and intersectional lenses of experiences sensitively but without apology (Collins, et al, 2021; Crenshaw, 1989). The diversity audit allowed us to do this work authentically. For example, in Linda's lesson Navigating Complicated Spaces, teachers are provided with resources to center race and gender intersectionally. Because of the diversity audit, within our conscious practice of cultural humility, coupled with acknowledging our Whiteness, we were able to purposefully center the Black artists and Black experiences in the Educator Resources, which are arranged in tandem with the exhibition themes of *Community & Memory*, *Hair Politics*, and *Black Joy*.

TEXTURES: THE HISTORY AND ART OF BLACK HAIR: AN EXEMPLAR OF *TESTIMONIO*

TEXTURES took place at Kent State University in Ohio, U.S. Kent State University is a state university located approximately 50 minutes southeast of Cleveland. The exhibit took place in the Kent State University Museum, open since 1985, a space dedicated to housing historical dress, fashion, textiles, and decorative arts from various places worldwide. It houses over 20,000 objects in its collection. Its viewership has been predominantly White.

Tameka Ellington conceptualized The TEXTURES exhibit, birthed by decades of experiences around what she coined as "texturism," or "the cultural capital of 'good hair' as it intersects with the social hierarchies of colorism" (Ellington & Underwood, 2020, p. 9). Ellington refers to colorism, a term first coined by Alice Walker in *In Search of Our Mothers' Gardens* and defines it as "the ideology that light-skin Blacks are more beautiful, more intelligent, and more civilized" (p. 16) than dark-skin Blacks.

Together with Joseph Underwood, Ellington co-curated the exhibition, which has to date received record attendance at the museum. TEXTURES addresses Black hair through art, materials, and visual culture, blending fine and vernacular art together, with over 200 objects. Alongside items from collections from legends in the Black hair industry, such as Madame C. J. Walker and Dr. Willie Morrow, and items from the Antebellum U.S. and pan-African societies, Black contemporary artists' works are juxtaposed alongside the artifacts to provide reactions and reflections to the various time periods of Black hair to help tell the stories.

Like Ellington, art educators Amelia Kraehe and Joni Boyd Acuff (2021) discuss their racialized experience of Black hair growing up. Acuff provides "*counter*visualities" (p. 51) for her daughter regarding Black hair and visual culture. Contemporary artists, confronting the ethics and politics of how images are made and perceived in society, contribute to a growing consciousness and discussion surrounding Black hair. Similarly, Ellington (in Ellington & Underwood, 2020) recounts four key "Hair traumas" that laid the groundwork for her research. She shared first person *testimonio* of her racialized and racist experiences she endured as a Black woman, "drawing on experiential, self-conscious, narrative practice to articulate an urgent voicing of something to which one bears witness" (Blackmer Reyes & Curry Rodríguez, 2012, p. 525).

"The objective of the *testimonio*," Reyes and Rodríguez (2012) assert, "is to bring to light a wrong, a point of view, or an urgent call for action. Thus, in this manner, the *testimonio* is different from the qualitative method of in-depth interviewing, oral history narration, prose, or spoken word. The *testimonio* is intentional and political" (p. 525). The TEXTURES exhibit itself became *testimonio*, illuminating the identity politics of hair in a society that attaches value to the texture of hair. TEXTURES is Ellington's powerful and transformative *testimonio* in disrupting the hegemony of texturism. What aligns Ellington's work with *testimonio*, as opposed to traditional Western memoir or personal narrative, is what Reyes and Rodríguez (2012) highlight: "We come to understand this form of writing as part of the struggle of people of color for educational rights and for the recovery of our knowledge production" (p. 526). TEXTURES become an embodiment of a space to engage in transformative thinking as part of visual *testimonio* strategies that resist hegemonic racist and oppressive practices associated with Black hair. In this paper, we are expanding this notion of *testimonio* to encompass the exhibition as a whole. TEXTURES as an exhibition disrupts the racist canon of the Whiteness of art history, serving as a powerful example of *testimonio* that not only names oppression (texturism) but serves to arrest its action (disrupt texturism and celebrate Black beauty).

CONCLUSION

Did we build a better curriculum than we have previously because of our shared experiences? Without hesitation, we both answer "yes." However, we are on shifting sands, not firmly planted; still filled with self-doubt in our Whiteness, still learning, still revising, still questioning, and absorbing needed perspective; and still hopeful for future collaborations to do better. The opportunity to engage with Tameka Ellington and Joseph Underwood, the Co-curators of TEXTURES, and with Christina Timmons, our graduate student and co-writer of the Educator Resources, and Curatorial Assistant of the TEXTURES exhibition [1], certainly built an authenticity that otherwise would have been lacking. Doing work outside of and within one's Whiteness to construct a curriculum in this way requires a level of cultural humility that takes time to develop. Deep listening and openness to lived experience outside of one's perspective and interpretations through dialogic interactions that emerge through building personal cultural humility, coupled with a critical race theory orientation and critical feminist race theory orientation, have the potential to empower art educators to construct better curriculum.

ACKNOLWEDGEMENTS

We would like to extend our sincerest gratitude to Dr. Tameka Ellington, Dr. Joseph Underwood, and Christina Timmons for their generous collaborative spirits during this curricular project.

REFERENCES

Acevedo, S. M., Aho, M., Cela, E., Chao, J., Garcia-Gonzales, I., MacLeod, A., Moutray, C., & Olague, C. (2015). Positionality as knowledge: From pedagogy to praxis. *Integral Review, 11*(1), 28–46.

Acuff, J. B. (2019). Editorial: Whiteness and art education. *Journal of Cultural Research in Art Education, 36*, 8–12.

Barone, T. (2001). *Touching Eternity: The Enduring Outcomes of Teaching.* Teachers College Press.

Broome, J. (2018, March). *Acknowledging academic privilege: Autoethnography, self reflection, and missteps leading to growth as a culturally sensitive educator.* Presentation at the National Art Education Association Convention, National Art Education Association, Seattle, WA.

Cahan, S., & Kocur, Z. (Eds.). (1996). *Contemporary art and multicultural education.* The New Museum of Contemporary Art.

Childers-McKee, C. D., & Hytten, K. (2017). Critical race feminism and the complex challenges of educational reform. *Urban Review, 47*, 393–412. DOI 10.1007/s11256-015-0323-z

Cisneros, N. (2021). Critical race theory, intersectionality, and feminist philosophy. In K. Q. Hall & Ásta (Eds.), *The Oxford handbook of feminist philosophy* (pp. 1–10). Oxford University Press. DOI: 10.1093/oxfordhb/9780190628925.013.41

Collins, P. H., Gonzaga da Silva, E. C., Ergun, E., Furseth, I., Bond, K. D., & Martínez-Palacios, J. (2021). Intersectionality as critical social theory. *Contemporary Political Theory, 20,* 690–725. https://doi.org/10.1057/s41296- 021-00490-0

Cosier, K. (2019). On Whiteness and becoming warm demanders. *Journal of Cultural Research in Art Education, 36,* 1–18.

Crenshaw, K. (1989). Demarginalising the intersection of race and sex: A Black feminist critique of antidiscrimination doctrine, feminist theory and antiracial politics. University of Chicago Law School, *University of Chicago Legal Forum, 1,* 139–167.

Danso, R. (2018). Cultural competence and cultural humility: A critical reflection on key cultural diversity concepts. *Journal of Social Work, 18*(4), 410–430. doi: 10.1177/1468017316654341

Delgado, R., & Stefancic, J. (2001). *Critical race theory: An introduction.* New York University Press.

Deliu, A., & Ilea, L. T. (2018). Combined and uneven feminism: Intersectional and postconstructivist tendencies. *Metacritic Journal for Comparative Studies and Theory, 4*(1), 5–21. doi: 10.24193/mjcst.2018.5.01

Dewhurst, M. (2019). Reflecting on a paradigm of solidarity? Moving from niceness to dismantle whiteness in art education. *Journal of Cultural Research in Art Education, 36,* 1–20.

Ellington, T. (2020). The conception of TEXTURES: The history and art of Black hair. In *TEXTURES: The history and art of Black hair* (pp. 13–17). Hirmer.

Ellington, T., & Underwood, J. (2020). The history and art of Black hair. *TEXTURES: The history and art of Black hair.* Hirmer.

Filbin, D. N. (2021). Discovering how black lives matter: Embracing student voice in the art room. *Art Education, 74*(1), 19–25.

Freire, P. (1992). *Pedagogy of the oppressed.* Continuum.

García, G. S. (2022). Foreword. In L. C. Sotomayor II (Ed.), *Teaching in/between: Curating educational spaces with autohistoria-teoría conocimiento* (pp. xvii–xxi). Vernon Press.

hooks, b. (1984). *Feminist theory from margin to center.* South End Press.

hooks, b. (1994). *Teaching to transgress: Education as the practice of freedom.* Routledge.

Kraehe, A. M., & Acuff, J. B. (2021). It's not just about hair: Visual education and the aesthetics of racism. *Art Education, 74*(2), 50–51.

Ladson-Billings, G. (2005). The evolving role of critical race theory in educational scholarship. *Race Ethnicity and Education, 8*(1), 115–119.

Ladson-Billings, G., & Tate, W. F. (1995). Toward a critical race theory of education. *Teachers College Record, 97,* 47–68.

Lippard, L. (2000). *Mixed blessings. New art in a multicultural America.* The New Press.

MacLeod, J. (1995). *Ain't no makin' it: Aspirations & attainment in a low-income neighborhood.* Westview Press.

New Museum (2011). *Rethinking contemporary art and multicultural education.* Routledge.

Nieto, S. (1992). *Affirming diversity: The sociopolitical context of multicultural education.* Longman.

Reyes, K. B., & Rodríguez, J. E. C. (2012). Testimonio: Origins, terms, and resources: *Equity & excellence in education, 45*(3), 525–538, DOI: 10.1080/10665684.2012.698571

Sleeter, C. E. (2016). Learning to work while white to challenge racism in higher education. In N. M. Joseph, C. Haynes, & F. Cobb (Eds.), *Interrogating whiteness and relinquishing power* (pp. 13–26). Peter Lang.

Spillane, S. (2015). The failure of whiteness in art education: A personal narrative informed by critical race theory. *Journal of Social Theory in Art Education, 35*(1), 57–68.

Spring, J. (1997). *Deculturalization and the struggle for equality: A brief history of the education of dominated cultures in the United States* (2nd Ed.). McGraw-Hill.

Verjee, B. (2012). Critical race feminism: A transformative vision for service-learning engagement. *Journal of Community Engagement and Scholarship, 5*(1), 57–69.

CHAPTER 15

BIPOC PERSPECTIVES AND SUBALTERN VOICES

The Doubly Oppressed Subject of the Marginalized Feminist Artist

Maia Toteva
Texas Tech University

BIPOC approaches in art education challenge established hierarchies and hegemonies by developing a pluralistic mindset, fostering solidarity, and advancing an ideascape for a better learning experience. Probing the linguistic strategy and conflicted reception of the new acronym, this essay explores the adoption of a BIPOC intersectional framework in the teaching and revision of a graduate seminar on feminist art which was modified to incorporate historically underrepresented and marginalized BIPOC artists, particularly oppressed and displaced female voices. The analysis of quantitative and qualitative survey data demonstrates that the course revisions led to a revitalization of the curriculum that increased student interest and satisfaction. Combined with (self)reflections on identity, a desire to un-learn privilege and bias, and endeavoring to promote a more inclusive language, the decolonization of the canon resulted in a more effective learning environment and the increased participation of diverse students who had felt disengaged or marginalized in previous academic discussions.

Keywords: College Teaching, BIPOC, Global Feminism, Art Education, Contemporary Feminist Art, Student Evaluations of Teaching, Intersectionalism

BIPOC: LANGUAGE, CRITIQUES, AND NEW PERSPECTIVES

The heightened racial tensions and social activism of recent decades have significantly increased the scrutiny of our pedagogical frameworks and language (Alim, 2016; Shashkevich, 2016).[1] Scholars and activists are calling for reexamination and decolonization of all terms and methodologies that privilege whiteness as part of the larger critique of European-centered canons, male-dominated perspectives, and other forms of oppression and discrimination (Crenshaw, 2018; Wing, 2003). Anti-subordination awareness and resistance are particularly instrumental in the era of massive crises, such as global pandemics and ecological disasters, in view of the fact that these calamities disproportionately impact marginalized populations and communities of color (Buchanan et al., 2020). Today, the fight for social justice has become a fight for inclusive terminology and unbiased curricula, as language and education not only reflect but also affect the ways in which the human mind structures and perceives the world, and present indispensable tools in the striving for a better society and community (Martin, 1991; Wing, 2003, p. 83).

Addressing recent controversies around the term "BIPOC" (Black, Indigenous, and People of Color), this essay explores the ramifications of the concept in the college classroom by focusing on its role in the teaching of global feminisms and visual art as a way of reexamining the art education curriculum through self-reflective practice and revisionist methodological frameworks. The case in point is a graduate seminar on contemporary feminist art, which I revised in order to incorporate a greater number of BIPOC female artists and writers and to integrate activities that promote inclusive language and pluralistic approaches. Based on the data from anonymous surveys, students in the class felt welcomed and appreciated as members of a diverse learning community—a positive outcome that was facilitated to a large extent by the preliminary session of guided self-reflective introductions and discussion that I created. While the inadequacies and limitations of the terminology, including the term BIPOC, were openly acknowledged and critiqued in class, learners coming from diverse backgrounds demonstrated an increased motivation to participate and share personal thoughts and experiences related to identity, art, and various forms of stratification.

The class discussion devoted a significant amount of scrutiny and attention to the labels and concepts used to center or describe intersectional identities. Since the primary goal of the course modifications was to highlight the work of feminist artists who remained underrepresented in the traditional canon and curriculum, such as Black and Indigenous women and, more generally, women of color, the

---

[1] The call for a new specialized field—raciolinguistics or LangCrit—focusing on and exploring the connection between race and language in discussed in Alim (2016).

term BIPOC received a primary consideration in the pedagogical critique and revision. Coined around 2013, the acronym BIPOC quickly attracted attention in the public sphere as a notable signpost positioned at the intersection between linguistic awareness and anti-subordination engagement (Garcia, 2020; The BIPOC project, n.d.).[2] Appearing first online, the new term gained rapid popularity on social media (WHO does the acronym "BIPOC" actually serve, n.d.). According to its critics, the acronym garnered support mostly among the "educated elites" who saw themselves as "progressive voices on issues of race or ethnicity, regardless of their identity backgrounds," but the concept has also faced mounting waves of criticism since the beginning of 2020 (Deo, 2021). Combining an unapologetic activist provocation with a controversial approach to centering and generalization, the term was destined to raise pressing questions about race, identity, and pedagogy in relation to language.

To start with its composition, phonetically, the acronym's alternation of consonants and vowels exercises a certain auditory appeal. BIPOC's melodious string of 5 initials is easily pronounced as 1 disyllable word, while its opaque semantics elicit the open invitation of an abbreviated riddle to any readers unfamiliar with the coinage's meaning.[3] Using analogous strategies, all initializations, abbreviations, and acronyms engender an attention-grabbing effect and present a potent pedagogical device, as they utilize a synecdochical relation between part and whole (letter and word) that prompts the reader to search for the most appropriate referent behind each component in the encoded composition. In addition, by interlinking a range of concepts into a condensed phrase, the acronyms entail inherent, though sometimes contentious, decisions about ordering, hierarchy, and intertwined semantic and syntagmatic connections. Bringing together 3 deeply felt categories related to inclusion, race, justice, and identity while making bold choices in regard to their grouping, (re)ordering, and priority, BIPOC is bound (and arguably designed) to stir controversies and evoke strong reactions. Therefore, it is to the pedagogical advantage of the educator to utilize the acronym's polemic approach as an edifying opportunity to reflect on larger social issues by way of posing pertinent questions.

The correlation between BIPOC's graphic components and their lexical referents is fairly straightforward—as mentioned above, the acronym stands for Black, Indigenous, (and) People of Color.[4] Beyond the direct correspondence between word and initial, however, the term generates a slew of problematic relations (Garcia, 2020).[5] Its encoded syntagma foregrounds and centers 2 of the 3 racial

---

[2] Traced to a single 2013 tweet, the exact origins of the term BIPOC remain unclear.
[3] Structured as riddles in terms of semantics, abbreviations, acronyms, and initialisms invite the reader to find the lexical entities that they evoke or refer to by way of convention.
[4] The capitalization of each category varies in different publications and on social media—from capitalizing all nouns in the phrase to eliminating any capitalization or capitalizing only "Indigenous."
[5] The punctuation and junctions linking the components of the phrase also vary, and such discrepancies can dramatically alter its semantics. The junction "and" is most often present between "Indigenous"

communities—Black and Indigenous (with a positional emphasis on Black)—by demarcating them as separate groups and placing them in the beginning of a tripartite series (Clarke, 2020).[6] At the same time, it lumps together all other non-white minorities into one umbrella category—People of Color—and places them at the end of the successive (and thus inherently hierarchical) arrangement (Grady, 2020).[7] As soon as these asymmetric relations enter the extralinguistic realm of social justice, marginalization, and racial privilege, BIPOC's unapologetic (re)ordering becomes even more problematic. Raising legitimate questions about the ways in which different identities are centered, generalized, excluded, or erased, the term faces challenges on multiple fronts and several trajectories of criticism that have framed it as damaging, failing, or at least unnecessary (Deo, 2021).

One of the primary arguments against BIPOC exploits the disjunction between language and the actual (extralinguistic) reality. According to this position, the term is not only deceptive but also harmful to the cause in the fight for social justice, as its use is detrimental to the resistance against systems of racial privilege. The underlying belief is that the acronym creates a false sense of unity and inclusion by prioritizing 2 marginalized groups *in name only* (by way of virtue signaling), while in fact those groups continue to remain peripheral or excluded (Deo, 2021). A variation of this critique asserts that BIPOC highlights 2 particular minorities—Black and Indigenous—within the category of People of Color, while in reality those communities are often ignored or left out of the dominant cultural discourse (Wade, 2020). In addition, discussions that take into account the social context in which the term has been evoked or employed also point out that the centering of those 2 groups makes sense in some situations, but it may not offer the best approach to confronting discrimination in other cases and circumstances (Kim, 1999).

According to a third line of critique, identity labels that bring together different categories and minorities can be useful when fostering a sense of solidarity, but they can also erase individual differences, silence subaltern voices, and enforce new hierarchies in order to encompass distinct communities under one common umbrella such as People of Color (Pérez, 2020). Finally, one of the most potent contestations that expose the limitations of BIPOC is presented by the praxis and methodology of intersectionalism which promotes a multifaceted approach to so-

---

and "People of Color" but is sometimes omitted, just as "and" is usually absent but can occasionally appear between "Black" and "Indigenous" in some versions of the statement. These seemingly minor distinctions can create substantial semantic disparities. For instance, the tripartite series in "Black, Indigenous, and People of Color" is far more encompassing than the bipartite "Black and Indigenous People of Color."

[6] As a linguistic unit, syntagma consists of language components (phonemes, letters, words, or phrases) that are arranged in a sequential relationship to one another.

[7] "People of Color" brings together under one umbrella category all those who are non-white, such as Black, Latinx/Xicanx, Asian American, and Indigenous People. Historically, such broad categories were used to create a sense of unity and solidarity.

cial phenomena and contends that issues of race intersect with problems of gender, class, sexuality, elitism, and so on (Crenshaw, 1991; hooks, 1984).[8] Thus, particular communities within the category "People of Color" may experience marginalization, exclusion, and domination differently from other groups evoked and lumped under the same designation. For instance, women of color can be "doubly oppressed" in a stratified, male-dominated society that privileges "whiteness," while Black queer women or Indigenous transgender people often face multiple, intersectional, and interrelated levels of subjugation and discrimination.[9] Therefore, the plight of such subgroups may require a special focus and methodology to avoid their erasure by BIPOC's broad approach and wide brushstroke.

BIPOC AND THE SUBALTERN FEMINIST ARTIST

As a timely cultural provocation with notable ramifications and failings, BIPOC can nonetheless be used effectively as part of the art curriculum, particularly if combined with other approaches, such as intersectionality, LGBTQ+ rights, and global feminisms, and especially when treated with a heightened degree of (self) reflection and willingness to un-learn entrenched privilege and bias.[10] Incorporated within such pluralistic pedagogical frameworks and praxis, BIPOC can generate resourceful topics for discussion, precisely because it raises uncomfortable questions and offers problematic solutions to multilayered concerns and social conditions. Transposing self-awareness to the foreground, I employed the term in the teaching and revision of a traditional European-centered graduate seminar on contemporary feminist art, which had been previously dominated by Western perspectives and white female artists.

As instructor of record, I altered the course content and structure in order to update its scope and methodology and to make the topic more appealing to a diverse, interdisciplinary, and socially engaged body of students. The modified seminar was taken by MAE and PhD students, including BIPOC and international learners, at a large HS PWI (Hispanic Serving Predominantly White Institution). BIPOC was one of the terms and frameworks discussed and scrutinized in class, while BIPOC language, issues, and perspectives became instrumental in the process of curriculum restructuring and revision. Students and educators reflected on the linguistic tactics and shortcomings of the acronym in comparison to other concepts and categories, as they pondered the multidimensional questions that the term engendered in relation to race, identity, and their individual artistic and pedagogical practice.

---

[8] "Intersectional feminism" looks beyond advancing the equality of men and women to confront the webs of interrelated forms of oppression such as racism, imperialism, colonialism, elitism, classicism, etc.

[9] On the "double oppression" of women of color, see Spivak (1988). The marginalization of Native American women is discussed in Sutton (1970).

[10] On global feminisms, see Reilly et al. (2007). The term "intersectionality" was arguably first introduced in Crenshaw (2018).

One of the BIPOC-related pedagogical strategies employed in the beginning of the semester (more specifically, during the first- and second-class meetings) involved personal introductions structured as guided reflections on issues of identity, gender, race, interculturalism, and more broadly, notions of belonging and not belonging. As a preparatory step, the students were invited to complete a thematic questionnaire (Appendix A) adapted from pedagogical sources by answering different sets of questions as a way to prompt (self)reflection and to structure each learner's introduction (Cahan & Kocur, 1995; Chang et al., 2019). Due to the sensitivity of the topic, the students were encouraged to respond to at least 3 questions of their choice in each section and to select which sections to focus on and utilize during their introduction to the class. Given the latitude of the approach, it became significant that all learners participated energetically in the class discussion and actively engaged with and responded to all parts of the questionnaire. In the process, the exercise prompted them to reflect on our inherent biases and to articulate their own perceptions of identity as well as to think about points of difference and commonality between themselves and their classmates.

In a post-module survey assessing the effectiveness of the approach, students shared that they felt welcomed, included, and encouraged to participate in the discussion after that (self)reflection exercise. The qualitative and quantitative data also demonstrated that the learners assumed a greater initiative and willingness to contribute to the dialogue, because they felt free to express their thoughts and opinions in class and better equipped to appreciate the diversity and identities of others, particularly their intersectional BIPOC peers. The results were also addressed in a post-module class discussion in which students presented their thoughts and vocalized some of the impressions and conclusions formed in the process of reflection. As numerous learners disclosed, they reached the common inference that they were all different and unique in terms of individual experience and identity, and at the same time they saw themselves as similar, connected, and united by a shared aspiration to feel respected and included as part of a larger learning community.

The most substantial changes linked to BIPOC and intersectionality involved revisions to the course structure which led to the adoption of an anti-essentialist, pluralistic feminist framework that encompassed marginalized communities and women of color not only in the West but also in South America, Africa, the Middle East, and Asia. Such pluralistic approaches challenge the monolithic model of Western feminism by highlighting Black and Indigenous voices and incorporating feminist art made in different parts of the world, particularly in oppressive, colonial, and postcolonial contexts. Students examined select works by BIPOC and non-Western artists and critics while tracing the erasure of minority subjects, as the discussion explored how those identities become marginalized by dominant ideologies, white privilege, and colonial agendas. For example, a module titled "Intersectionality and Black Subjectivity: Towards a Black Feminist Visuality" enabled students to experience the silenced perspective of displaced female voices and to perform an intersectional Black critique of visual canons marked by oppression and stratification.

The experiential learning practiced in such modules fosters solidarity and resistance by inviting immersion in the marginalized existence of Black, Indigenous, and minority women who are objectified, spoken for, or presented as Other in both discourses—African-Americanists focusing on African-American men and Euro-American feminists focusing on Euro-American women.[11] These displaced feminist voices embody the subaltern perspectives of non-Western and non-white women as "doubly colonized" subjects; i.e., objects exploited by both foreign colonizers and the local male-dominated order (Spivak, 1988). Highlighting the oppressed Black and Indigenous selves and, more broadly, the intersectional experiences of women of color, the revised curriculum incorporated the anti-subordination aspiration and spirit of BIPOC, while acknowledging the acronym's inadequacies and limitations. In the end, the pedagogical exercise of course review and revision as well as the student reception of the modified seminar demonstrated that, while our language and methodologies are by no means a finished or impeccable project, a critical reflection on their deficiencies, flaws, and potentialities can bring learners and educators closer to a shared appreciation of diversity, inclusion, and understanding.

In conclusion, the revisionist incorporation of BIPOC feminist artists and intersectional methods revitalized the old curriculum and increased student interest and satisfaction. Combined with (self)reflections on identity, a desire to un-learn privilege and bias, and endeavoring to promote a more inclusive language, the decolonization of the canon resulted in a more effective learning environment that increased the participation of diverse students who had felt disengaged or marginalized in previous academic discussions. Therefore, when integrated in a pluralistic pedagogical framework that involves a multiplicity of approaches such as intersectionality and global feminisms, the centering of silenced voices and displaced identities could offer a path to greater inclusivity and solidarity inside and outside of the classroom.

APPENDIX A
STUDENT INTRODUCTIONS:
INTERSECTIONAL REFLECTION QUESTIONNAIRE

Adapted from Chang et al. (2018) and Cahan and Kocur (1995).

I. Please Share Some Information About Yourself:

1. Name (preferred name or nickname)
2. Area/program/field of study?
3. Concentration/interests/dissertation topic?

---

[11] On Black feminism, see Tesfagiorgis (1993), Dickerson et al. (1982), Harris (1990), and MacKinnon (1991).

4. Aspirations in life?
5. What do you plan to do after graduating?
6. Background in/experience with global feminism/feminist art?

II. **Think about Your Childhood:**

1. How was I expected to behave because of my race or gender?
2. How have my parents, family members, classmates/peers, and romantic interests influenced my beliefs about race and gender?
3. How did I come to define my identity?
4. What makes one feel like they belong?
5. Do you feel like you are different from the people around you? Why or why not?
6. Are you different by choice or do you feel like the society, norms, the way you look, etc. force you to be different or to be seen as different?
7. Do you try to conform to the norms and expectations of society, and would you rather be different?
8. What do/would you do to conform? What do/would you do to stay true to yourself?
9. What do you think about people who are different and do not want to follow the predominant norms or expectations?

III. **Personal Background Questions (Societal Norms Impact):**

1. How do different identity markers such as race, ethnicity, (dis)ability (as differently abled), body size, socioeconomic status/class, sexual orientation, gender, spirituality/religion, or other characteristics*, influence my identity? (e.g. ethnicity/culture's influence on notions of masculinity/femininity; religion and binary gender norms, etc.) *use any that may apply.
2. How have I benefited from adhering to social or identity expectations/roles?
3. When I did not conform to such expectations/roles, what were the consequences?
4. Do I experience stressors in relation to my identity?
5. Have I experienced fluidity regarding my gender/race? (e.g., someone identifying as female and engaging in male-dominated sports or wearing men's clothing)
6. Has my gender/race ever been misidentified (e.g. attaching my voice to a different gender; assuming my race/gender just by learning my name)? How did that feel?

IV. **Personal Background Questions (Gender Norms Reinforcement):**
   1. How have I contributed to reinforcing binary gender socialization? (e.g., making jokes, participating in gender reveal parties, imposing traditional gender norms on my loved ones, etc.)
   2. Do I use he/she, men/women in my writing and verbal communications as a catch-all way to describe "everyone"? Why?
   3. What thoughts and feelings arise when I cannot easily determine the gender of a person? Do I find myself trying to determine the sex assigned at birth?
   4. How do I feel about being asked to use or corrected to use non-binary pronouns (they/them etc.)?
   5. When a person challenges societal binaries in any way (e.g., with appearance, speech, by advocating for non-conforming gender identities, etc.), how do I feel? What automatic reactions does this evoke?
   6. Have I assigned traditional male/female names that match the biological sex of my pets/baby/newborn? Why? Do I socialize my pets/baby/newborn based on gender (e.g., pink collar for a girl)? Why might it be important to me that a person be able to identify the gender of my pets/baby/newborn?

V. **Discussion Questions for General Reflection:**
   1. What are the most important things that you learned about your classmates?
   2. What are the most surprising things that you learned about your classmates?
   3. How does this knowledge help you better understand yourself and your classmates?
   4. Describe any unexpected *similarities* between classmates of different backgrounds.
   5. Explain how your classmates represent diversity and why you think (or don't think) diversity/inclusivity is valuable and enriching.
   6. How can we apply that knowledge to our thinking about feminist art and our professional practice?

REFERENCES

Alim, H. S. (2016). Introducing raciolinguistics: Racing language and languaging race in hyperracial times. In H. S. Alim, J. R. Rickford, & A. F. Ball (Eds.), *Raciolinguistics: How language shapes our ideas about race* (pp. 1–30). Oxford University Press.

The BIPOC project. (n.d.). Retrieved May 26, 2022, from https://www.thebipocproject.org/.

Buchanan, L., Bui, Q., & Patel, J. K. (2020, July 3). Black lives matter may be the largest movement in U.S. history. *The New York Times*. Retrieved May 26, 2022. Retrieved from: https://www.nytimes.com/interactive/2020/07/03/us/george-floyd-protests-crowd- size.html

Cahan, S., & Kocur, Z. (1995). *Contemporary art and multicultural education*. Routledge.

Chang, S. C., Singh, A. A., & Dickey, L. M. (2019). *A clinician's guide to gender-affirming care: Working with transgender and gender-nonconforming clients*. New Harbinger Publications.

Clarke, C. (2020, September 19). BIPOC: What does it mean and where does it come from? CBS News. Retrieved May 27, 2022, from https://www.cbsnews.com/news/bipoc-meaning- where-does-it-come-from-2020-04-02/

Crenshaw, K. (1991). Mapping the margins: Intersectionality, identity politics, and violence against women of color. *Stanford Law Review*, *43*(6), 1241. https://doi.org/10.2307/1229039

Crenshaw, K. (2018). Demarginalizing the intersection of race and sex: A black feminist critique of antidiscrimination doctrine, feminist theory, and antiracist politics [1989]. *Feminist Legal Theory*, 57–80. https://doi.org/10.4324/9780429500480-5

Deo, M. E. (2021). Why BIPOC fails. *Virginia Law Review Online*, *107*, 115–142. https://heinonline.org/HOL/LandingPage?handle=hein.journals/inbrf107&div=9&id=&page=

Dickerson, D. P., Hull, G. T., Scott, P. B., & Smith, B. (1982). All the women are white, all the blacks are men, but some of us are brave—black women's studies. *The Journal of Negro Education*, *51*(3), 361. https://doi.org/10.2307/2294703

Garcia, S. E. (2020, June 15). Where did BIPOC come from? *The New York Times*. Retrieved May 26, 2022, from https://www.nytimes.com/article/what-is-bipoc.html

Grady, C. (2020, June 30). *Why the term "BIPOC" is so complicated, explained by linguists*. Vox. Retrieved May 27, 2022, from https://www.vox.com/2020/6/30/21300294/bipoc- what-does-it-mean-critical-race-linguistics-jonathan-rosa-deandra-miles-hercules

Harris, A. P. (1990). Race and essentialism in feminist legal theory. *Stanford Law Review*, *42*(3), 581. https://doi.org/10.2307/1228886

hooks, b. (1984). *Feminist theory: From margin to center*. South End Press.

Kim, C. J. (1999). The racial triangulation of Asian Americans. *Politics and Society*, *27*(1), 105–138.

MacKinnon, C. A. (1991). From practice to theory, or what is a white woman anyway? In C. A. MacKinnon (Ed.), *Women's lives, men's laws* (pp. 22–31). Harvard University Press. https://doi.org/10.2307/j.ctv1pdrpw3.6

Martin, B. L. (1991). From negro to black to African American: The power of names and naming. *Political Science Quarterly*, *106*(1), 83. https://doi.org/10.2307/2152175

Pérez, E. (2020). (MIS)calculations, psychological mechanisms, and the future politics of people of color. *The Journal of Race, Ethnicity, and Politics*, *6*(1), 33–55. https://doi.org/10.1017/rep.2020.37

Reilly, M., Nochlin, L., Brooklyn Museum, & Davis Museum Cultural Center. (2007). *Global feminisms: New directions in contemporary art*. Merrell; Brooklyn Museum.

Shashkevich, A. (2016, December 27). *Stanford experts highlight link between language and race in new book*. Stanford News. Retrieved May 26, 2022, https://news.stanford.edu/2016/12/27/link-language-race-new-book/

Spivak, G. C. (1988). Can the subaltern speak? In C. Nelson & L. Grossberg (Eds.), *Marxism and the interpretation of culture* (pp. 271–313). University of Illinois Press.

Sutton, V. (1970, January 1). *Guest post: Native American exclusion as a form of paper genocide*. TTU DSpace Home. Retrieved May 27, 2022, from https://ttu- ir.tdl.org/handle/2346/86530

Tesfagiorgis, F. H. W. (1993). In search of a discourse and critique/s that center the art of black women artists. In A. P. A. Busia & S. M. James (Eds.), *Theorizing Black feminisms: The visionary pragmatism of Black women* (pp. 228–267). Routledge

Wade, L. (2020, September 24). Covid-19 data on Native Americans is 'a national disgrace.' This scientist is fighting to be counted. *Science*. Retrieved May 27, 2022, from https://www.science.org/content/article/covid-19-data-native-americans-national- disgrace-scientist-fighting-be-counted

WHO does the acronym "BIPOC" actually serve?: The takeaway. WNYC Studios. (2020, June 25). Retrieved May 26, 2022, from https://www.wnycstudios.org/podcasts/takeaway/segments/acronym-bipoc-race- language

Wing, A. K. (2003). *Critical race feminism: A reader*. New York University Press.

CHAPTER 16

DISRUPTING AND TRANSGRESSING THE CANON

Including BIPOC Voices

Rochonda L. Nenonene, Novea A. McIntosh, and R. Darden Bradshaw
University of Dayton

In this paper, three female faculty preparing future educators share singular and collective experiences and intentional action steps to challenge the reproduction of racist practices in teacher education influencing candidates and reinforcing the marginalization and oppression of students of color in schools. These traditional actions include the selection process for candidates and field sites, curriculum design, as well as selection of texts and readings by scholars that center whiteness, patriarchy and heteronormativity. We begin by examining and sharing the intersectionality of our identities as women, mothers, and educators. Within this context, at our Predominantly White Institution (PWI), we work, individually in our courses, and collectively in our programs, to dismantle and transgress the cannon. By empowering future educators through inclusion of authors from the non-western cannon, the implementation of critical pedagogy, and space for counter narratives we find spaces of healing, and potential disruption.

We are teacher educators. Three cis-gender faculty women. One, African American. One, Afro Caribbean Immigrant. One, White and Queer. All marginalized by virtue of race, gender identity, sexuality, or sense of othering and not belonging. All committed to dismantling structures, policies, and teacher preparation curricula that centers whiteness and maintains institutional racism (Picower, 2021). Here we share singular and collective experiences and intentional action steps to challenge the reproduction of racist practices in teacher education that influence candidates and reinforce the marginalization and oppression of students of color in schools. These traditional actions include the selection process for candidates and field sites, curriculum design, as well as selection of texts and readings by scholars that center whiteness, patriarchy and heteronormativity. We have committed to disrupting such practices; yet we feel the weight of this work. We engage in these spaces, advocating and working for change—taking up Lorde's charge—we will no longer "use the Master's tools" (1984, p.110).

As faculty women in a private, Catholic, Marianist[1] predominantly White institution (PWI), we witness the manufacturing of teacher candidates who graduate with limited cultural competence and a sense of superiority associated with their role as teacher in relation to students of color (Matias et al., 2017) and students who identify as LBGTQIA+ (Sadowski, 2017). This perpetuation of privilege, limits the educational achievement of the students viewed as deficit (Ladson-Billings, 1995). We have power and opportunity to be change agents. Ultimately, we hope and seek to develop culturally responsive educators who view themselves as social justice advocates (Love, 2019; Paris & Alim, 2014) in solidarity with the students and families they serve.

THREE EDUCATORS

African American

The intersections of my racial identity, feminism, and motherhood converge with my vocation and form the foundation of my commitment to help transform schools into safe, protective and equitable spaces for my children, and the 49 percent of Latino, African American, Asian, and Indigenous (NCES, 2021) students. My urgency stems from the fact that American schooling continues the marginalization of BIPOC through excessively high suspension rates of Black and Latinx students (Wood et al., 2021); unequal access to honors and advanced placement classes (Patrick et al., 2019); and the continued lack of resources and insufficient recognition of the contributions of American Native students' heritage and culture (Hussar et al., 2020).

The educational experiences I navigated as student, educator, and mother demonstrate that schools, proclaiming to offer the best educational opportunities to all, operate to protect practices centering whiteness while relegating students of color to a limited or substandard education. No matter the setting, urban or suburban, I

---

[1] The Society of Mary was founded in 1817. The Marianist educate for formation in faith; provide an integral quality education; educate in family spirit; educate for service, justice, peace, and integrity of creation; and educate for adaptation and change (Characteristics of Marianist Universities, 2019).

have witnessed how teachers' deficit perceptions and schools' policies and procedures facilitate racism and oppression of Black students (Nenonene et al., 2021) under the guise of upholding rigorous educational expectations.

Teacher preparation, long criticized for the maintenance of structures and policies favoring white, middle-class expectations of schooling (Ladson-Billings, 1998; Milner & Howard, 2004) have failed to substantially change selection and preparation of teacher candidates, utilizing normative standards that simultaneously privilege and oppress. For example, relatively unchallenged are standardized admissions tests, like *Praxis*. Considered best practice and required by accreditation boards, these historically had a negative impact on the selection of candidates of color (Feuer et al., 2013). Paradoxically calls persist to increase diversity in the teaching profession, matching the steadily increasing ethnic and linguistic diversity of America's student population.

Another element, common to many educator preparation programs (EPP), is curriculum devoid of intellectual frameworks or epistemologies outside of the standard western norms regarding child development and pedagogical practices. Essentially, the perspectives, voices and contributions of Black, Indigenous, and People of Color (BIPOC) remain largely absent from the training of future educators. This fosters unfounded assumptions that there are no equivalent theoretical understandings as important as those birthed in western ideology.

The two examples reflect a small fraction of the collective practices that enable EPP to protect and replicate whiteness. Our profession fails to admit those who could bring in diverse perspectives and, once admitted, neglects to offer an education that should provide candidates with knowledge, understandings, and experiences that eliminate bias, honor all cultures, and promote equitable academic outcome for students. I will not aid my profession in this endeavor. Therefore, I persist and disrupt in spaces where I have the ability to effect change.

AfroCaribbean

As an AfroCaribbean scholar practitioner, my educational experience has evolved from a colonial Eurocentric beginning to a decolonized Afrocentric becoming. Intentionally finding my voice and learning myself, I explore the works of my ancestors, the invisible scholars in the canon. 'I am liminal because I am black but always questioning' (Wynter, 2015) and finding truths. I learned early I will be marginalized and live as the 'other' within my native country, still a patriarchal space with lasting structures of colonialism. I also understood as an immigrant in predominantly White world, I am the 'other' and even amongst my own Black people, secondarily marginalized (Crenshaw, 1989). I am displaced and continue to be, hence my activism grows.

I chose to advocate for students with complex multiple identities because I share such experiences. Marianist educators—valuing both faith and reason—educate for adaptation and change while embracing the rich cultural differences present in the community to stimulate meaningful dialogue in and out of the classroom (Association of Marianist Universities, 2019). My formation is rife with challenges but framed with possibilities. Caribbean immigrants "are caught in… the immigrant-navigating-a-new-society world, … a racialized black world, and an unaccepting white world" (Louis et al., 2020, p. 112). Here I am afforded to be my true self: to give voice to the marginalized and underserved in wider parts of the world, a necessary part of remaking our lives (Warner, 2012) as I disrupt the canon through 'human emancipation' (Wynter, 2015), a transgression correctly representing the 'others.' Preparing preservice teachers to teach diverse student populations, I purposefully focus on identifying, naming, dismantling the canon to locate myself within the discourse, and challenge predominantly white students fixated on their whiteness.

As the parent of a Black boy, I dread the slow violence and marginalization he faces, noted by Wright and Ford (2019), in schools living and growing up with an assumption of criminality by virtue of his race. I am shocked by these racialized characterizations of boys as "lazy, violent, athletic, thug…"(p.19). My patriarchal culture was the opposite. Men were often more celebrated and elevated, even in schools. I use my identity and legacy to inculcate in my son a "rejection of negative Black stereotypes and their replacement with notions of empowerment, beauty, and assertiveness" (Fournillier & Lewis, 2010, p. 11). Taking a long view of education from P-12 spaces to higher education (PWI), I evolve as a disrupter, protecting his life and that of so many BIPOC students, as an educator of the teachers who will change their lives, either with grief or gain. I contend it must be the latter for every student in the classroom.

White and Queer

Educated in a system that I never questioned, my teachers looked like me; whiteness was the standard of measure. As an out LGBTQ+ college student my interest in queer theory became the gap I named in my own education. Foucault (1980) noted heterosexuality cannot exist without homosexuality; in fact, homosexuality defines heterosexuality—creating a binary dialectic—of one being normal, the other abnormal, transforming sexuality, like the construction of race, to a social and cultural concept (Denzin & Lincoln, 2000; Kraehe & Acuff, 2021). Challenging the discourse around sexuality and gender—and thereby, altering existing power relations (Butler, 2010) queer theory moves away from static identities to identities as constructed from various contexts in which we live (Shelton, 2018). Yet, even in troubling heterosexism, I did not see that queer theory, in deconstructing power, was situated primarily in whiteness and White experience, omitting considerations of race.

Like many White people, I was acutely unaware how whiteness put me at an advantage. In my EPP, concepts of "multiculturalism" and inclusion, aimed toward social justice, filtered through a white supremacist lens fostering a reductionist pedagogical approach (Wilson, 2018) perpetuated an "othering" stance. In art education, like U.S. education, White females far outnumbering male and female teachers of color are often unprepared to teach in urban, public schools while student makeup in K–12 schools is more economically, socially, racially, and ethnically diverse than ever before; "educators, across the country, most of whom are White...are without an important interpretive framework to help them understand their interactions with students, or even their cross-racial interactions with colleagues" (Tatum, 1997/2017, p. 75). Well prepared to teach K–12 art and completely unprepared to teach culturally responsive art, I was the statistic to which Dr. Tatum refers. Teaching in a primarily Latinx community and simultaneously raising our Black daughter who did not see herself reflected in school, I recognized this gap and began interrogating my miseducation (Angulo, 2016).

That miseducation and community led me here. I hoped to educate future art teachers in culturally responsive pedagogy and critical racial literacy (Kraehe & Acuff, 2021). I was excited my daughter, one of four Black people in her high school class would finally see herself racially reflected. However, while racially diverse, this new city was geographically and economically segregated. This PWI sits at the intersection of that divide with an art education EPP firmly entrenched in centering art education through an outdated, one pointed cannon celebrating White, male, and western artists *as* worthy of study. Art education reflects larger society; it is "susceptible to reproducing racial hierarchies in ways that, consciously or unconsciously, maintain or exacerbate racial inequality" (Kraehe & Acuff, 2021, p. 38). The relationship of my mothering influenced my conceptions of how to prepare future art teachers. Challenging racist approaches and transitioning art education required holding a mirror up to what I was taught.

In parenting a young Black woman, I recognized moments of dissonance and missteps where internalized and unexamined whiteness perpetuate personal and systemic racism and insulated me. And as a teacher of future teachers, I know students entering the field will be teaching students who look more like my daughter than me. I see the way my grandson is transformed from the precious child he is to a threat. The relationship between a Black boy's early learning years and the adverse treatment he receives as an adolescent (Wint, et al., 2021) reifies negative assumptions and educational actions toward Black boys. When a smart, quirky and talented young man is seen as Black first, and a learner second he is limited. This reductionist construct is grounded in reinforcing race as a means of holding power. I too had been socialized in the fiction of "seeing" race as based in biology and not, as it really is, a social construction "born of the human imagination and put into practice by people" (Kraehe & Acuff, 2021, p. 16).

Students choose this school for a variety of reasons. Almost all suggest it ties to how they feel on campus—the sense of community that is perceived. But who feels community on a PWI campus? How does unexamined whiteness impact and perpetuate spaces ripe for continued white supremacy? I persist. Using my privilege to trouble the margins of art education teacher preparation and supporting future teachers in becoming anti-racist art educators, thus redefining 'community.'

EXAMINING OUR INTERSECTIONALITIES

As colleagues we draw upon our experiences as individuals to intentionally and collectively explore positionalities in relation to the marriage between teacher education and whiteness (Matias et al., 2017). Interestingly, while each experienced structures which celebrated our identities, we work in a space where community is touted, whiteness is centered, and minoritized voices are excluded. Marginalized as women, we each have lived another layer of exclusion. As women and parents of Black children who need to see themselves represented in educational spaces, we urgently act to disrupt structures perpetuating white privilege, naturalization, xenophobia, white racialization, and colorblindness (Matias, 2016). These attributes, when weaponized, harm our students of color.

The practices and policies of higher education, formed in a world impacted by racial thinking continue a white dominant space. Privileging exists in the form of admittance tied to historically biased assessments designed to exclude BIPOC students; high tuition costs; low number of faculty of color; an insidious cycle of efforts to recruit diverse students but failure to adequately support and retain them to graduation; and the tension that exists between the guise of exclusionary practices, grounded in theology, which offer a conditional welcome and inclusion in community. We are aware that the intractable history of whiteness and the institutional ramifications of white supremacy must be interrupted.

EDUCATION WITH WHITENESS AT THE CENTER

We seek to nurture BIPOC students in spaces where they flourish without pretext or tokenism (Emdin, 2021). We interrogate our identities as we prepare candidates focusing on retention of our BIPOC and LGBTQ+ students. Confronting the exclusionary cycle of EPP leads to an understanding that beliefs and practices are a direct result of a myriad of things: cultural heritage, faith, sexuality, schooling experiences, and in particular the formal training received in teacher preparation promoting the hegemony of whiteness. In response, we have modified curriculum to include the intellectual traditions, research, and pedagogies that are grounded in culture, community, and collectivism; intentionally sought opportunities to impact institutional policies and practices that favor whiteness; and importantly, provided safe spaces for BIPOC candidates to express themselves, and assist them as they navigate a PWI. We do our best when we stand in the gap advocating for anti-racists practices and EPP reform promoting culturally responsive educators.

DISRUPTION WITHIN THE MARGINS

Transgressing the cannon means disruption from entrance through graduation. Our students have been educated in a visual culture reflecting White teachers 'saving' the non-White students (think Freedom Writers, Dangerous Minds, etc.). Unintentionally exacerbated and born out of the idealism of service associated with Catholicism, we reframe through a reciprocal service lens resulting in mutually beneficial exchange. Many may go back to their communities to teach and live; by laying the groundwork we hope they will not revert to the default; instead shifting "the metaphor of the good teacher as helper to the good teacher as abolitionist" (Love, 2019).

Awakenings and Introductions

Students arrive at my introduction to the profession course with apolitical concepts of teaching never considering teaching as an act of social justice. Yet, Nieto (2006) notes that schools are political, "because it's about power: who has it, who makes the key decisions that affect people's lives—or not—and who benefits from these decisions" (p.5). Positioning teaching as an act of resistance and liberation reframes the discourse.

Constructs such as equity, inclusion and opportunity gaps have not yet entered the lexicon of these candidates. Confronted with these new realities we explore how school systems contribute to the exclusion of students. They come to see the importance of culturally sustaining practices by studying the actions and policies of exemplary schools dedicated to achievement of all students served.

Vital to the disruption of the cannon is the inclusion of authors from non-western intellectual traditions offering perspectives that challenge, elicit reflection and enable candidates to consider the origin of practices and the impact on students. This reframing leads to difficult questions and necessary discussions that force the recognition of the replication of privilege and awakening to understandings that can change mindsets and dismantle barriers that are rooted in racism.

Finally, initial field placements occur in schools where students of color, immigrant, and multilingual learners are the majority population. As a result, candidates demonstrate an increasing interest in teaching in urban schools and dispositions that indicate movement towards being culturally competent.

Unsettling Diversity Education in White Spaces

As a diversity and assessment professor, my classroom community is grounded in critical pedagogy explicitly leading to alternative epistemologies, legitimizing what counts as knowledge (Hill Collins, 2013), hence the explicit works of minority scholars are integrated in my courses. Students are engaged in critical reflection of the historical trauma (Sotero, 2006) BIPOC students continue to face in modern day classrooms including testing, used as another tool of whiteness and systemic oppression to exclude students of color from the dominant culture. Students spend time interrogating themselves, privilege, power, and whiteness as they gauge their intercultural competence and actively seek to improve their continuous learning: interpersonal engagement and hardiness helps build relationships; and bridges the cultural dissonance between BIPOC students and White teachers. Using a critical lens of sociocultural perspectives, students learn nontraditional assessment practices that engage diverse students to embrace their productive struggles, cultivate perseverance, and a growth mindset.

Wright and Counsell (2018) noted that to disrupt the pipeline and restore childhood innocence, more equitable and culturally responsive efforts are needed to celebrate and heal BIPOC students. Critical race theory with culturally responsive pedagogy (Ladson-Billings, 1995) builds preservice teacher's dispositions that supersedes mundane teaching acts (Howard, 2012) giving voice to antiracist teaching (Kendi, 2019), abolitionist teaching (Love, 2019) and decolonizing and culturally relevant pedagogy (McCarty & Lee, 2014) exposing the trauma but give healing strategies to support students' social and emotional needs. Students navigate uncharted territories far removed from their histories and narratives, exploring BIPOC stories and using these tools to challenge scripted and culture-blind curriculums (Wright & Ford, 2019). We transgress the canon as a conduit to advocate for equitable teaching and assessment focused on supporting and monitoring implementation of teaching practices that build from students' cultural funds of knowledge, practices, and identity resources (Esteban-Guitart & Moll, 2014).

Queering Art Educator Preparation

Creating spaces for counter narratives (Lee, 2012) alters hegemonic paradigms within EPP's, therefore, I focus on queering art education—to *trouble*: to challenge the position of normative identities and experiences in EPP at a PWI; in that queering we "dismantle the dynamics of power and privilege persisting around diverse subjectivities" (Young, 2012, p. 127).

Queering is iterative across all four years of preparation. For instance, when first year students recall the artists they learned in their K–12 art education it is rare, although not unheard of, for them to list any BIPOC or LGBTQ+ artists. We deconstruct why their knowledge base is skewed heavily toward White, Western European male artists. A sense of community includes seeing yourself reflected in the world—not just physically, but in curriculum. Student knowledge is deepened in anti-racist pedagogy through currere, art integration and texts written by non-White art educators, including Kraehe and Acuff's critically important text *Race & Art Education*. Using Emdin's (2016) pedagogical approach of reality pedagogy, grounded in culturally relevant pedagogy (Ladson-Billings & Tate, 1995) future teachers consider the cultural background of students, seeing the influence of cultural identity. These tangible tools for action lead to transformative learning.

Students, first unsure what is necessary to be an anti-racist educator address how they have unknowingly and unconsciously enjoyed and benefited (McIntosh, 1988) from privilege and acknowledge what must be unlearned. We strive to create Crum & Hendricks' 'brave spaces; we uncover personal hidden narratives that may be racist, gendered, or otherwise problematic (Acuff, 2018); we explore counternarratives of teachers of color in PWI spaces empathizing with what it might be like to be a BIPOC student taught by a teacher unaware of their own whiteness. Anticipating they will participate in the historical struggle for racial and social justice in K–12 art education, we use modeling, discourse, and invitation into the discomfort, examining white supremacy, questioning internalized and accepted narratives while interrogating ways in which racism is taught through visual literacy and art education.

Disruption Leads to Healing

Teacher actions and words, negative or positive, leave indelible imprints on the spirit and psyche of students. We are a profession entrusted with what many would call our countries' most valuable resource, our children. Left unchecked, this power, this ability to mold greatness or do great harm in obvious and imperceptible insidious ways can crush souls, destroy dreams and shatter spirits.

In shifting these practices, we heal, as individuals, as educators, as a community. Healing occurs by defining a new default. Sharing counter narratives, we see greater representation of self; moments of unlearning lead to empathy and solidarity. While the injection of alternative epistemologies and critical pedagogy in white spaces come with risk it also fosters healing as we continuously reflect with an inward gaze (Paris & Alim, 2014). hooks noted to counter complicity of the default White dominance, we must have more narratives of barriers broken down, coalitions formed, and solidarity shared. It is within this "woman space" (hooks, 1994, p. 110) we find healing as we represent our true selves and find the promise of this work.

REFERENCES

Acuff, J. (2018). Confronting racial battle fatigue and comforting my blackness as an educator. *Multicultural Perspectives, 20*(3), 174–181.

Angulo, A. J. (2016). *Miseducation: A history of ignorance-making in America and abroad.* Johns Hopkins University Press.

Association of Marianist Universities. (2019). *Characteristics of Marianist universities.* https://marianistuniversities.org/wp-content/uploads/2019/10/CMU_2019_FINAL.pdf

Butler, J. (2010). *Gender trouble* (8th ed.). Routledge.

Crenshaw, K. (1989). Demarginalizing the intersection of race and sex: A Black feminist critique of antidiscrimination doctrine, feminist theory and anti-racist politics. *University of Chicago Legal Forum, 1989,* 139–167.

Denzin, N. K., & Lincoln, Y. (2000). *The handbook of qualitative research.* (2nd ed.). SAGE.

Emdin, C. (2016). *For White folks who teach in the hood…and the rest of y'all too: Reality pedgagoy and Urban education.* Beacon Press.

Emdin, C. (2021). *Ratchedemic.* Beacon Press.

Esteban-Guitart, M., & Moll, L. (2014). Funds of identity: A new concept based on the funds of knowledge approach. *Culture & Psychology, 20*(1), 31–48.

Feuer, M. J., Floden, R. E., Chudowsky, N., & Ahn, J. (2013). *Evaluation of teacher preparation programs: Purposes, methods, and policy options.* National Academy of Education.

Foucault, M. (1980). *The history of sexuality Volume I: An introduction.* (Hurley Trans.). Vintage Press.

Fournillier, J. B., & Lewis, T. (2010). Finding voice: Two Afro Caribbean immigrant members of the academy writing 'home.' *Studies in Continuing Education, 32*(2), 147–162. DOI: 10.1080/0158037X.2010.488356

Hill Collins, P. (2013). *On Intellectual Activism*. Temple University Press.

hooks, b. (1994). *Teaching to transgress: Education as the practices of freedom*. Routledge.

Howard, T. (2012). Culturally responsive pedagogy. In *Encyclopedia of diversity in education*. (Vol. 1, pp. 550–552). Sage Publications, Inc.

Hussar, B., Zhang, J., Hein, S., Wang, K., Roberts, A. P., Cui, J., Smith, M., Mann, F. B., Barmer, A., & Dilig, R. (2020). *The condition of education 2020*. NCES 2020-144. National Center for Education Statistics. https://nces.ed.gov/pubsearch/pubsinfo.asp?pubid=2020144

Kendi, I. (2019). *How to be an anti-racist*. Penguin Random House.

Kraehe, A. M., & Acuff, J. B. (2021). *Race and art education*. Davis.

Ladson-Billings, G. (1995). Toward a theory of culturally relevant pedagogy. *American Educational Research Journal, 32*(3), 465–491.

Ladson-Billings, G. (1998). Just what is critical race theory and what's it doing in a nice field like education? *International Journal of Qualitative Studies in Education, 11*(1), 7–24.

Ladson-Billings, G., & Tate, W. (1995). Toward a critical race theory of art education. *Teachers College Record, 97*(1), 47–68.

Lee, N. (2012). Culturally responsive teaching for 21st-century art education: Examining race in a studio art experience. *Art Education, 65*(5), 48–53.

Lorde, A. (1984). *Sister outsider: Essays and speeches*. Crossing Press.

Louis, D. A., Thompson, K.V., Staney, C.A & Louis Jr., B. M. (2020). Reflections, relationships and immigrant contributions: Narratives of Afro-Caribbean faculty members in American higher education. *Caribbean Educational Research Journal 5*(1), 110–130.

Love, B. (2019). *We want to do more than survive: Abolitionist teaching and the pursuit of educational freedom*. Beacon Press.

Matias, C. E. (2016). *Feeling white: Whiteness, emotionality, and education*. Sense Publishers.

Matias, C. Nishi, N., & Sarcedo, G. (2017). Teacher education and whiteness and whiteness in teacher education in the United States. *Oxford encyclopedia*. https://doi.org/10.1093/acrefore/9780190264093.013.279

McCarty, T., & Lee, T. (2014). Critical culturally sustaining/revitalizing pedagogy and Indigenous education sovereignty. *Harvard Educational Review, 84*(1), 101–124.

McIntosh, P. (1988). White privilege: Unpacking the invisible knapsack. Excerpted from working paper 189. *White privilege and male privilege: A personal account of coming to see correspondences through work in women's studies*. Wellesley College Center for Research on Women.

Milner, R., & Howard, T. (2004). Black teachers, Black students, Black communities: Perspectives and insights from experts. *The Journal of Negro Education, 73*(3), 285–297.

National Center for Educational Statistics. (2021). *Racial and ethnic enrollment in public schools*. https://nces.ed.gov/programs/coe/indicator/cge

Nenonene, R., McIntosh, N., & Vasquez, R. (2021). Faculty of color and collective memory work: An examination of intersectionality, privilege and marginalization. *Understanding and Dismantling Privilege, XI*(2), 1–21.

Nieto, S. (2006). *Teaching for social justice in schools: Stories of courage and corazón* [Conference Presentation]. National Council of Teachers of English Assembly for Research, Chicago IL.

Paris, D., & Alim, H. S. (2014). What are we seeking to sustain through culturally sustaining pedagogy? A loving critique forward. *Harvard Educational Review, 84*(1), 85–100.

Patrick, K., Socol, A., & Morgan, I. (2019). Inequities in advanced coursework: What's driving them and what leaders can do. *Education Trust*. https://edtrust.org/resource/inequities-in-advanced-coursework/

Picower, B. (2021). *Reading, writing and racism: Disrupting whiteness in teacher education and in the classroom.* Beacon Press.

Sadowski, M. (2017). More than a safe space: How schools can enable LGBTQ students to thrive. *American Educator,* (Winter 2016–2017), 4–9, 42.

Shelton, S. (2018). "We're in the freaking Bible Belt" A narrative analysis of the complexities of addressing LGBTQ topics while teaching in the Deep South. In K. Strunk (Eds), *Queering education in the Deep South,* (pp. 3–14). Information Age Publishing.

Sotero, M. (2006). A conceptual model of historical trauma: Implications for public health practice and research. *Journal of Health Disparities Research and Practice, 1*(1), 93–108.

Tatum, B. D. (1997/2017). *Why are all the Black kids sitting together in the cafeteria? And other conversations about race.* Basic Books.

Warner, O. (2012). Black in America too: Afro-Caribbean immigrants. *Social and Economic Studies, 61*(4), 69–103.

Wilson, G. (2018). Global consciousness in art education: Utility and problematics of curriculum development within a critical postmodern relational praxis. *Journal of Cultural Research in Art Education, 35*(1), 13–25.

Wint, K. M., Opara, I., Gordon, R., & Brooms, D. (2021). Countering educational disparities among Black boys and Black adolescent boys from pre-K to high school: A life course-intersectional perspective. *Urban Review.* https://doi.org/10.1007/s11256-021-00616-z

Wood, L. J., Harris, F., Howard, T., Mohamed, Q., Essien, I., King, T., & Valentin, E. (2021). *Suspending or future: How inequitable disciplinary practices disenfranshise Black kids in California's public schools.* Black Minds Matter Coalition. http://bmmcoalition.com/suspendingourfuture/

Wright, B., & Counsell, S. (2018). *The brilliance of Black boys: Cultivating school success in the early grades.* Teachers College Press.

Wright, B., & Ford, D. (2019). Remixing and reimagining the early childhood school experiences of brilliant Black boys. *Boyhood Studies, 12*(1), 17–37. doi: 10.3167/bhs.2019.120103

Wynter, S. (2015). *On being human as praxis.* Duke University Press.

Young, T. (2012). Queering "the human situation." *Journal of Feminist Studies in Religion, 28*(1), 126–131.

CHAPTER 17

RECLAIMING OUR INDIGENEITY

Deconstructing Settler Myths Through Micro-Activism

Rosalva Resendiz, Lucas Enrique Espinoza, and Luis Enrique Espinoza
Univeristy of Texas Rio Grand Valley

Colonization, imperialism and white patriarchal settler myths within our family are very much part of traditional familism of the Latinx/Mexican American/Chicanx community. To deconstruct oppressive familial colonial traditions, we propose a critical framework which situates our auto/biographies on the borderlands historically, as well as our experiences towards a Mestiza Consciousness, by using intersectionality/matrix of domination as a lens. Living on the borderlands, our physical closeness to Mexico helps us maintain close ties to family, customs and language. But even then, we live with internalized prejudice against our own indigeneity. In order to deconstruct oppressive family structures from within, we propose a self-exploration into our indigenous roots, as well as a deconstruction of settler myths by providing a short history of the borderlands from the perspective of Chicanx Indigenous Mestizos/as.

It is always difficult to begin our story when we have spent a lifetime living on the border of our identity, as insiders/outsiders in our homelands. We have learned to live/survive at the margins/intersections of the matrix of domination (Collins, 1990/2015), to survive/resist under colonial-imperialist structures of oppression, fighting for the right to be and simply exist in our homelands, which have been conquered and divided. Our goal is to provide a critical pedagogy of micro-activism to help deconstruct the settler myths that have dominated our lives as Hispanic/Latin American/Mexican American/Chicanx Indigenous people. Micro-activism is an individual-level effort for community-building action to drive change, challenge assumptions and shape the cultural identity of a group (Marichal, 2013). Our identity is complex and framed by patriarchal White supremacy, making our journey towards self-actualization more difficult, especially when colorism is considered. This aligns with the decolonial feminist goal of recognizing oppression and resources to resist oppression/subjugation/domination.

As indigenous people of the Tejas/Tamaulipecan/Coahuiltecan/Mexico borderlands, we have been doubly conquered, first by Spain and then by the United States (Miller, 1980). The river that was known as Ganapetuan by the Coahuiltecans and the Rio Bravo by the Spaniards and Mexicans, became the Rio Grande River (Lovett et al., 2014), separating the peoples of the region from their families. Unfortunately, our stories have been lost in the history and the narratives of colonial administrators, treated as footnotes and claiming our extinction, as we continue to thrive against a system of White supremacy. Thus, we seek to share our journey towards decolonization to encourage fellow educators/advocates and community members to help our families heal from the generational traumas we have lived by being forced to accept Eurocentric Christian patriarchal cultural norms and values of racism, colorism, classism, and sexism.

As social justice scholars, we lead the resistance through our pedagogy, research, and service. We are committed to deconstructing the ideological hegemony which maintains systems of inequality and discrimination. To do this, we must use critical race theory towards decolonizing the personal, and communal to empower people of color in the Americas, where systemic oppression continues to harm BIPOC through policies and dominant socio-cultural practices (Delgado & Stefancic, 2012). Many of our indigenous and Mestizo/a people hold stereotypes of inferiority, placing whiteness and assimilation as a goal, viewing whiteness as beautiful and our brown/copper-colored skin as shameful evidence of our indigeneity.

We must contest all frameworks which have separated us from our ancestors across time and space. The Indians in Mexico and the "Native Americans" in the U.S. are the same people regardless of man-made boundaries and government extermination policies. We need to change the language we use when fighting for our right to be in our homelands. We are not immigrants. We are indigenous to these lands. We are natives. Our ancestral mothers were conquered/raped into submission until we lost our languages and became a society of displaced mestizos, without a tribe and extinct/erased in the eyes of the ruling governments.

A SHORT STORY OF COLONIZATION/GENOCIDE: MILITARIZATION OF THE TEXAS/MEXICO BORDER

It is imperative to teach history from a critical perspective to decolonize the sociopolitical narratives that have erased the history of colonial/imperialist genocide (Dunbar-Ortiz, 2021). In 2019, Patrick Crusius, a domestic terrorist from North Texas drove to the border town of El Paso and massacred 22 Mexican Americans, fueled by Trump's anti-immigration rhetoric (The United States Department of Justice, 2020). In his manifesto, Crusius explained that his actions were a direct response to the Hispanic invasion of the U.S., very much ignorant or in denial that the borderlands were the homeland of the indigenous mestizo Mexican Americans.

As BIPOC educators, it is imperative to teach beyond the University classroom as it creates action/change for the community, our families, and ourselves. For many of us, our families do not always understand what we study, research, and/or write. We deconstruct and share our historical knowledge/research with our community, beginning with our own families (Smith, 1999/2012). History is written by the conquerors and therefore, they have positioned themselves as the bringers of civilization while ignoring the genocide. In 1492, Christopher Columbus was found by the Arawaks and labeled them *Indios* (Hulme, 1986). The horrors of this first contact were forgotten, and Columbus Day was established to honor this human trafficker.

History has romanticized the unions of White European conquistadors and indigenous women, although they were gifted, raped, and trafficked. With the "mixing" of races, a caste system was set up in New Spain, with Spaniards at the top. Towards the north of the Aztec Empire, the semi-nomadic Chichimeca Indians fought against the Spaniards and resisted their expansion into their territories until the Spanish Crown took a different approach by bribing them into submission (Miller, 1985). By the 1740s, José de Escandon was given the task to colonize *El Seno Mexicano* (Gulf Coast area) or what was to become *Nuevo Santander*. Escandon had been an Indian killer and because of his successes was given the task to subdue the native population of South Texas and Tamaulipas (Miller, 1980). Today, a statue of Escandon stands in front of The University of Texas Rio Grande Valley, while the decimation of the Indian population is not marked/acknowledged (López, 2014).

In 1820, Mexico won its independence from Spain and allowed Anglos to settle in the Tejas area. By 1836, Anglos stole the land in order to maintain slavery, which had been outlawed by the Mexican government. Finally, in 1848, the U.S. defeated Mexico, stole more than half of its land, annexed Texas and established the Rio Grande River as a boundary. The Border Patrol was created in the 1900s, as the Texas Rangers roamed the border lynching both mestizos and Indians and called this series of raids the Bandit Wars. However, there were no bandits (Chipman & Joseph, 1992/2010; Martinez, 1988).

Across the Rio Grande Valley, there are remnants of our conquest, symbols of war scattered across. We grew up knowing that we were conquered people, with relics of cannons of the Mexican American War sitting quietly on Paredes Line, in a city named after Major Jacob Brown, whose fort stands by the international bridge, still claiming an imaginary Tejas boundary. One hundred miles from the international boundary, we have federal checkpoints that monitor our movements to the North, as well as to the West and East.

As children, we were aware that the Border Patrol were federal agents looking for *mojados*. We were aware that we were privileged to be U.S. citizens, but we also knew that the color of our skin marked us as indigenous even when we were not allowed to identify with our indigeneity because we were Mexican.

THE MASTER'S TOOLS

For the master's tools will never dismantle the master's house. . . they will never enable us to bring about genuine change. (Lorde, 1984/2007, p. 112)

I have pondered this idea since I was in graduate school. Although the Liberal Tradition is Eurocentric, it has merit in that it has advocated for truth, reason, and freedom. And from the ideals set forth by the Enlightenment, Western thought developed/progressed as a scorpion with a curved tail under threat, ignoring indigenous knowledge and philosophy as primitive and savage, ready to strike against any who contests White supremacy. Nevertheless, as we have joined the ranks of academia, we have been part of the progression and evolution of the institutions towards an uneasy compromise that negotiates power carefully to maintain systemic racism and sexism.

By the time we graduated from high school, we had been assimilated into the U.S. American values and the myth of the American dream, along with its claims of freedom and justice. We soon encountered institutional racism, sexism, and classism within the University system. But we also came across scholars who critiqued academia for failing to teach democratic ideals which were meant to propel our society towards an inclusive society of equality, freedom, and justice (Anzaldúa, 1987; Collins, 1990/2015; Du Bois, 1994; Mills, 1959).

In our women's studies courses, we were introduced to critical race feminism and scholars such as Crenshaw (intersectionality), Collins (matrix of domination), and Anzaldúa (mestiza consciousness). It is from these scholars that we have derived inspiration for our decolonizing practices. It is at the intersection of auto/biography and history where we have situated ourselves to develop a sociological imagination utilizing the matrix of domination as a critical lens (Anzaldúa, 1987; Collins, 1990/2015; Collins, 1998; Crenshaw, 1989).

CONTESTING WHITE SUPREMACY: DECOLONIZING OUR IDENTITIES

Decolonizing begins with critically analyzing our Chicanx Mestizo/a identity and addressing the racism within the Hispanic/Latinx/Mexican American community. To reclaim our indigeneity, our journey begins with deconstructing the settler myths of White superiority, which we have reproduced in the Tejas/Mexico borderlands. We reclaim our lands by countering the hegemonic narratives of migration and extinction.

As indigenous people of this land, our activism begins with decolonizing ourselves and our family, which perpetuates systemic oppression by reproducing hierarchies through "traditional" values taught within the family which in part are Eurocentric. Settler myths are very much part of the traditional familism of the Mexican American community. As children, we learn our place in society based on sexist, racist, and classist schemas. Within the family, we have learned the settler myths of the "savage" dark Indian and the "civilized" white saviors. It is within the family, we find pride in a Spanish European last name, making us feel that we are worthy as descendants of conquerors. To deconstruct oppressive familial colonial traditions, we begin our analysis using the matrix of domination or intersectionality (Collins, 1998).

The process of decolonization/resistance has inadvertently always existed alongside colonization, as elements of our indigenous past remain in our language and culture. We refuse to forget. Although many of us have lost our native tongues, within the Spanish language many of our native words have survived, just as many of our indigenous cultural values. Spanish colonization and imperialist U.S. Americanization have indoctrinated us with internalized racism/colonialism. We have accepted hierarchies that privilege and place white over brown, English over Spanish, citizen over undocumented, male over female, rich over poor. We understand that all these prejudices are part of us, but instead of rejecting them, we embrace them and attempt to live under the burden of settler myths.

Every family has customs influenced by colonization and indigenous resistance. The customs we hold so dear are the result of compromises, resistance, and survival. In order to deconstruct oppressive family structures from within, we need to analyze and educate our own family through a decolonizing lens. The Spanish caste system left a culture of White supremacy which continues to harm BIPOC in the U.S. and Latin America. We grow up knowing that there is a privilege with light skin and although we have brown skin, we must distance ourselves from the indigenous. Those with light skin and colored eyes are seen as beautiful while being dark is associated with ugliness, poverty, and inferiority. We hear our family tell us to stay out of the sun so that we won't get darker. We are told that we need to marry someone lighter to *mejorar la raza*. If we are too indigenous, we have the mark of the *nopal en la frente*. In the borderlands, Mexican nationals call us *pochos* for being Mexican American and not fluent in Spanish, the language of the conquerors. We are told to be proud of our Spanish ancestry and ashamed of our Indigenous and African ancestry.

DECOLONIZING THROUGH MICRO-ACTIVISM

As residents of the borderlands, we have faced prejudice for being too Mexican, too Indian, and too Americanized. Living on the militarized borderlands can be frightening, especially for the undocumented. We are hyper-aware that to be free from scrutiny by agents of the government, it is in our best interest to assimilate, but that can be difficult when our brown skin gives us away.

Deconstructing colonial narratives begins with the individual. As educators, we must become micro-activists and refute/resist/deconstruct the settler myths. Decolonizing our borders begins with decolonizing our Mestizo/a identity and addressing the racism within the Mexican American community. We need to learn about our indigeneity. We need to learn to love our brownness, our *nopal en la frente*, instead of claiming European descent to establish our worthiness. In reclaiming our indigeneity, we reclaim our lands as natives. We must change the narrative of migration as we confront our indigenous identity with pride and not shame.

We begin this journey by learning history through a critical lens, by examining the systems of exploitation/repression/subjugation, from imperialism, to capitalism, racism and sexism. As we deconstruct internalized colonialism, we need to include our families in this journey. It is within the family that we have learned the settler myths of the "savage" dark Indian and the "civilized" white saviors. It is within the family that we find pride in a European last name, to validate our existence in the hierarchy. Our activism must begin with our own family, which perpetuates systemic oppression for our people.

Part of this journey involves analyzing and understanding our identity labels and the politics involved in our ethnic identity. What was your first understanding of ethnicity/race/nationality/citizenship? As bell hooks (1984) states, the personal is political and how we identify has implications beyond our personal life. The term Hispanic places Spanish ancestry as primary as it erases our indigeneity. Latinx has the same implications, yet all the countries colonized by the Spaniards are now referred to as Latin America under a term that has romanticized our heritage as Latin speakers, negating our indigenous languages and cultural diversity. As Mexican Americans, we recognize our Mexican ancestry, but fail to see that the name is a derivative from the indigenous *Meshicas* which also erases our African ancestry (León Portilla, 1959). Acknowledging our *mestizaje* can also be political, seen as the forced creation of the so-called "cosmic race," erasing the violence that our ancestors survived as we faced ethnic cleansing through the whitening of our people (Anzaldúa, 1987). For those of us that have lost our connections to our tribes and language, as displaced people in the U.S., we have embraced the term Chicanx to bring to the forefront our resistance to White supremacy and our pride in our indigenous ancestry. We must learn to love ourselves by resisting patriarchal White supremacy.

Most importantly, you must establish a dialogue with your elders and learn your stories. For many of us, our elders are part of the working class with limited access to higher education. Regardless of their educational levels, our elders carry on our oral family history. Ask them to remember and share, but also share your knowledge and educate them about internalized colonialism. We must remember that our elders have also been victims of colonization and have reproduced that trauma within our families, from alcoholism to violence and sexual violence/ abuse. We must critically engage with our elders to (re)educate them to help them heal. As you search for your indigenous roots, you will have to follow back the origin story your parents/elders have told you. The focus should not be on trying to link yourself to your European ancestry in the form of your last name, but to find the indigenous lands from where your ancestors came from. Although we have been displaced many times, we move with our nameless tribes and continuously return to our indigenous homelands.

Deconstructing Cultural Myths of Colonialism

To deconstruct oppressive familial traditions, we must situate ourselves at the intersections of our auto/biography and history. Using the concept of the matrix of domination as a lens to analyze the structure of the cultural values within your family, we can explore what family values are racist, classist, and sexist. We must confront the patriarchal values which are embedded in Mexican familism, silencing the female, and relegating her to a sexual object.

Within those patriarchal values, we have recreated hierarchies of Eurocentric White supremacy, privileging the whiteness in our families, and downplaying/ hiding *lo indio, moreno,* and *negro*. We use color to distinguish class, which is a legacy of the Spanish caste system. We idolize colored eyes over brown eyes. We create terms of endearment for our light skin daughters and sons: *la güera, el güero*. And knowingly label our dark children negatively as *prietos*. In Mexico as well as in the U.S., light skin people are treated with respect, while those of us with dark skin are ignored and belittled.

The epitome of Latin American/Mexican American beauty is Eurocentric and clearly depicted in Latin American *telenovelas*/soap operas, whereas the indigenous people barely exist in that realm. Due to the Spanish caste system and patriarchy, the Mexican White male and female are relegated to the upper class, while *Mestizos*, Indians, and Africans are expected to remain in their place as second and/or third-class citizens. To be light skin results in opportunities for social class movement, while those of darker skin are steered to agricultural labor. Expressions of these intersections are seen in the colonial narratives of parlor games such as *La Loteria*, with images of a menacing Apache Indian holding a weapon, *El Negrito* as a diminutive entertainer, the cultured White *Dama*/Lady, and the cultured White *Catrin*/Gentleman as examples of the civilized Mexican (Don Clemente juego de loteria, est. 1887).

As Chicanx indigenous people, there are many layers to our subjugation. Doing decolonial work requires a personal commitment to truth and justice which begins with us. The journey towards finding and liberating your indigenous self won't be easy as we contest the colonial and imperialist narratives. We need to begin by acknowledging that we are the descendants of the indigenous people of the Americas. We were conquered/colonized by the Spanish, but we have always resisted against our erasure. Many of us have lost our native tongues and tribes, but in the Mexican American family, we still carry the oral history and customs of our people. Furthermore, we need to remind and teach those around us that the Rio Grande River was not always a boundary. We were conquered by U.S. imperialism and our heritage was re-imagined without acknowledging our indigenous ancestry as if the Native Americans in the U.S. are not the same people as the Mexican Indians.

The U.S. continues to wage war on indigenous people, with practices of blood quantum to be formally recognized as native (Gutierrez, 2016). These practices negate the ancestry of Latin Americans and Mexican Americans as indigenous, labeling them immigrants in their own homelands, while the real immigrants are white. White colonizers have dominated the narratives and claimed our homelands as theirs based on the ridiculous notion of the Doctrine of Discovery (Dunbar-Ortiz, 2021).

In the U.S., we were not allowed to call ourselves Native Americans. Yet we are indigenous, but not Indian enough (Cotera & Saldaña-Portillo, 2014). The eugenics of racial purity has been utilized as a colonial imperialist method of erasing the original stewards of the Americas, by erasing the descendants of the Natives, the original Amerindians. The Spanish conquest established a caste system in which the purity of European ancestry set a racial standard of White superiority to the inferiority of the savage Indian and/or African (Menchaca, 2001; Saldaña-Portillo, 2016). While the imperialist U.S. established a caste system of indigenous purity as a way to erase all claims of indigenous Mexican mestizos, to label them immigrants in their homelands (Gutierrez, 2016). We must contest those narratives and find ourselves beyond the labels of colonialism and imperialism.

Decolonization requires us to immerse ourselves in the oral history and archival records of our people. We have provided a set of general guidelines that can assist in this process of educating ourselves, our families, and creating social change. It is through this process that we inform ourselves and help others to find who 'they' are and where 'they' come from.

1. Find your indigenous self. Start with critically analyzing your labels of ethnic/racial identification.
2. How has your knowledge of self been framed by colonization, settler colonialism, and imperialism? How has the racism, sexism, and classism

of colonialism and imperialism affected your identity and position within the Eurocentric patriarchy?
3. Speak with elders. Through these conversations, you will uncover the family stories and secrets.
4. Begin a formal genealogical search of your ancestry. Take note of the Mesoamerican regional origins of the family.
5. Research the migration patterns of your family.
6. Research the indigenous land colonized/settled by your Spanish ancestors.
7. Educate yourselves on Afro/Indigeneity knowledge and colonialism.
8. Look for teaching moments to share your findings with the family.

Decolonial work requires patience, especially with our families as we must (re)educate them about our indigenous history, colonization, and genocide. It is through this micro-activism that we can learn about our pre-Columbian roots. We need to teach everyone that we were never discovered. We are the descendants of empires, federations, tribes, and clans. We lived in spiritual connection with the land and the animals while studying the stars and the cycle of time. We had cities and villages. We had agriculture and irrigation systems. We were priests and priestesses. As educators, we must remember that beginning this decolonial experience can create discomfort when deconstructing one's own history. We must do this with patience and respect, for our elders are also victims with their respective scars and traumas.

REFERENCES

Anzaldúa, G. (1987). *Borderlands/La frontera: The new mestiza*. Aunt Lute Books.
Collins, P. H. (1990/2015). *Black feminist thought: Knowledge, consciousness and the politics of empowerment* (2nd ed). Routledge.
Collins, P. H. (1998). *Fighting words: Black women and the search for justice*. University of Minnesota Press.
Chipman, D. E., & Joseph, H. D. (1992/2010). *Spanish Texas, 1519–1821: Revised edition*. University of Texas Press.
Cotera, M. E., & Saldaña-Portillo, M. J. (2014). Indigenous but not Indian? Chicana/os and the politics of indigeneity. In *The world of indigenous North America* (pp. 575–594). Routledge.
Delgado, R., & Stefancic, J. (2012). *Critical race theory: An introduction* (2nd ed.). New York University Press.
Don Clemente juego de loteria. (est. 1887). *Mexican bingo set* [Card game]. Pastatiempos Gallo.
Du Bois, W. E. B. (1994). *Dusk of dawn: An essay toward an autobiography of race concept*. Transaction Publishers.
Dunbar-Ortiz, R. (2021). *Not a nation of immigrants: Settler colonialism, white supremacy, and a history of erasure and exclusion*. Beacon Press.
Gutierrez, G. (2016). Identity erasure and demographic impacts of the Spanish caste system of the indigenous populations of Mexico. In C. M. Cameron, P. Kelton, & A.

C. Swedlund (Eds.), *Beyond germs: Native depopulation in North America* (pp. 119–145). University of Arizona Press.

hooks, b. (1984). *Feminist theory: From margin to center*. South End Press.

Hulme, P. (1986). *Colonial encounters: Europe and the native Caribbean, 1492–1797*. Methuen.

León Portilla, M. (1959). Visión *de los vencidos*. Epublibre.

López, J. A. (2014, December 7). *López: The string of pearls of the Lower Rio Grande*. https://riograndeguardian.com/l%C3%B3pez-the-string-of-pearls-of-the-lower-rio-grande/

Lorde, A. (1984/2007). *Sister outsider: Essays and speeches*. Crossing Press.

Lovett, B. L., Gonzalez, J. L., Garza, R. B., & Skowronek, R. (2014). *Native American Peoples of South Texas*. Community Historical Archaeology Project with Schools Program.

Marichal, J. (2013). Political Facebook groups: Micro-activism and the Digital Front Stage. *First Monday*, *18*(12), 1–7. https://doi.org/10.5210/fm.v18i12.4653

Martinez, O. J. (1988). *Troublesome border*. University of Arizona Press.

Menchaca, M. (2001). *Recovering history, constructing race: The Indian, Black and White roots of Mexican Americans*. University of Texas Press.

Miller, H. (1980). *Jose de Escandon: Colonizer of Nuevo Santander*. The New Santander Press.

Miller, R. R. (1985). *Mexico: A history*. University of Oklahoma Press.

Mills, C. W. (1959). *The sociological imagination*. Oxford University Press.

Saldaña-Portillo, M. J. (2016). *Indian given: Racial Geographies across Mexico and the United States*. Duke University Press.

Smith, L. T. (1999/2012). *Decolonizing methodologies: Research and indigenous peoples* (2nd ed.). Bloomsbury Publishing.

The United States Department of Justice. (2020, February 6). *Texas man charged with federal hate crimes and firearm offenses related to August 3, 2019, mass-shooting in El Paso*. Office of Public Affairs. https://www.justice.gov/opa/pr/texas-man-charged-federal-hate-crimes-and-firearm-offenses-related-august-3-2019-mass

CONTRIBUTORS

Kristin Alder is a professor of Women's and Gender Studies at Texas Tech University and earned a Ph.D. in Multicultural Women's and Gender Studies from Texas Woman's University. Her work focuses on the work and theories of Gloria Anzaldúa.

Indira Bailey is an Assistant Professor of Art Education at Claflin University. She earned a dual-title doctorate in Art Education and Women's, Gender, & Sexuality Studies from The Pennsylvania State University, a BFA in Communication Design from Pratt Institute, a MA in Educational Leadership and Supervision from Kean University. She has over 20 years of teaching experience in the K-12 sector and community art programs. Bailey's research specializes in anti-racism, race and gender inequity, curriculum development, and the underrepresentation of Black artists. She draws on Black feminist thought, critical race feminism, outsider-within positionality, and social justice theory to create an inclusive and diverse curriculum. You can see Bailey's artwork at www.ibdesignstudio.com

Kelvin K. Boakye, since immigrating to the U.S. from Ghana when he was nine years old, Kelvin Boakye has been living in El Paso. He is a first-year pre-med student at Texas Tech University with a major in Psychology and he plans to double minor in Women and Gender Studies and Chemistry. Upon receiving his bachelor's degree, Kelvin Plans to attend Texas Tech University Health Sciences Center School of Medicine. Kelvin is currently a member of the Texas Tech Black Student Association and Minority Association of Pre-medical students. He hopes to one day be the Chief of Cardiology at a Major United States Hospital.

R. Darden Bradshaw is Associate Professor of Art Education and Area Coordinator for Art Education in the Department of Art & Design at the University of Dayton. She holds both a PhD in Art History and Education and an MFA in Fiber Art from the University of Arizona, Tucson, AZ. Her scholarship focuses on art integration, empathy development through arts, and the role of visual journaling as anti-racist pedagogy in the training of preservice teachers.

Esther Medina De León, an Associate Librarian at Texas Tech University Libraries has a MLS from the University of North Texas, Denton, and BA in Humanities from Lubbock Christian University. Her interests include Hispanic/Latinx culture, heritage, literature, and identity. She serves as a Women's & Gender Studies Affliated Faculty, a Leaders Engaged in Advancing Diversity (L.E.A.D) Fellow; on the advisory board for the Centers for Mexican American & Latino Studies and Latin American & Iberian Studies; ad primary investigator (PI) of the Chicana/x Latina/x Working Group, which serves to continue research and create dialog on the influence of Chicana and Latina feminisms.

Juliann B. Dorff, a Kent State University senior lecturer, is past-president of NAEA Special Needs in Art Education and past-president of CEC Division of the Visual and Performing Arts Education. She was awarded the 2019 NAEA/SNAE/VSA Beverly Levett Gerber Lifetime Achievement Award. She has received the Outstanding Teaching Award from KSU. She co-authored four editions of *VSA Teacher Resource Guides: A Series of Visual Art Lesson Plans Designed to Engage Students with Disabilities* published by the Kennedy Center and was an invited author for *The Handbook of Arts Education and Special Education and Art for Children Experiencing Psychological Trauma.*

Lucas Espinoza is faculty in the Department of Criminal Justice at The University of Texas Rio Grande Valley. He earned a Ph.D. in Sociology from Texas Woman's University and identifies as Chicanx Mestizo. His research area examines violence and resistance around Social Justice/Rights & Issues, Latinx Disparities, Victimology, Gender/Women's Studies and Culture. Dr. Espinoza is originally from the Rio Grande Valley, with more than seven generations on the borderlands and indigenous roots from both Mexico and the United States.

Luis Espinoza is faculty at The University of Texas Rio Grande Valley, with a Ph.D. in Sociology from Texas Woman's University. Additionally, he holds a Master of Public Health in Epidemiology from The University of North Texas Health Science Center and certifications in health education and public health.

Luis' research interests lie in Latinx/Mexican American health equity and social justice, particularly in women's health, disaster response/access, and health policy. Dr. Espinoza is originally from the Tejas borderlands and identifies as Chicanx Mestizo.

Addyson Frattura is a PhD Candidate in the Department of Educational Studies at the University of British Columbia. Addyson is a philosopher of education who studies school expulsion, abolitionist education, and ethics of love through philosophical, literary, and artistic traditions. She is particularly committed to addressing the question of human freedom and human suffering through writing and teaching in community.

Christen Sperry García is originally from the San Diego/Tijuana borderlands and her work is informed by Latina/x, Chicana/x, and borderlands theories. García is co-founder of the Nationwide Museum Mascot Project (NWMMP) that has performed at over 40 art museums and galleries including Museo de Arte Contemporáneo Lima, Peru; Museo Jumex, Mexico City; Museum of Contemporary Art San Diego, CA; Hammer Museum, Los Angeles, CA; and Museo de Arte Moderno, Bogotá, Colombia. García has published in peer-reviewed journals including *Art Education, The Drama Review,* and *Visual Arts Research.* She is an assistant professor in the School of Art at the University of Texas Rio Grande Valley.

Lourdes Garcia is a visual artist and art educator from South Texas where she lives with her husband, two children and three cats. She received her Bachelor's Degree in Graphic Design at Universidad del Noreste in Mexico. She holds a Teaching Certificate in Art K–12. She is currently in her last year of a MFA program in Visual Art at UTRGV in Edinburg, TX.

Elizabeth Gonzalez was born and raised in the lower Rio Grande Valley, Texas, considered the 956, El Rio Grande, El Valle. Her work is a personal narrative/visual testimonio on family stories, cultural identity, history, language, border culture, and the community that surrounds the Rio Grande Valley. Her use of textiles, terra cotta, paint, wood, and installation artworks center around personal observations of the Rio Grande Valley. She then completes the process by applying media that references Mexican American culture. Her works have been exhibited in juried exhibitions in the United States-Icons and Symbols of the Borderland Exhibit (2018), 5th Annual Mujer-Eres International Art Exhibition (2019), UTRGV-Brownsville Rusteberg Art Gallery (2019), Rising Eyes of Texas (2021) and received an honorable mention for best in 3D work. Currently, she is attending the University of Texas Rio Grande Valley to pursue an MFA with a Certificate in Mexican American Studies.

Meghan L. Green, M Ed., is a 4th grade teacher at Uplift Ascend Primary in Fort Worth, TX as well as an Adjunct Professor of Early Childhood Studies at the University of North Texas. She is also currently a doctoral candidate studying Curriculum and Instruction with a specialization in Early Childhood Education at Texas A & M University-Commerce. Ms. Green earned her B.A. in Anthropology with a minor in African American studies from Howard University and an Ed. M. in Early Childhood Education from Northwestern State University. Ms. Green's scholarship centers Black feminist thought within early childhood settings.

Chloe Grace Ferrer is a first-year student at Texas Tech University from the Houston area. She is majoring in Marketing at the Rawls College of Business and minoring in Women's and Gender Studies. Upon completion of her bachelor's degrees, she will market for a global nonprofit. Chloe was a part of The Leadership Institute in the Fall of 2021 and is currently a member of Women in Business and Kappa Delta sorority where she serves an Appointed Officer position as a member of the Philanthropy and Community Service Team.

Rocio Guerrero is a Mexican multi-media artist from South Texas, Rio Grande Valley, she is currently attending the University of Texas Rio Grande Valley, College of Fine Arts pursuing her master's in fine arts in Spring 2022. She is an Art educator in Hidalgo, Texas where she has been teaching Visual Arts at Hidalgo Early College High School for five years. Her work focuses on appreciating women's strength in a dialog and other modernistic traditions. Her most recent works consist of a series *Figuras de Mujeres* about women's identity representing the essence of women's narratives of feminine sensuality, beauty, and strength. Her work proposes a vision beyond the male gaze, signing a richer context of existence for the feminine within the human condition.

Eunkyung Hwang is a dual-title Ph.D. candidate in Art Education and Women's, Gender, and Sexuality Studies at The Pennsylvania State University. Eunkyung has been an elementary school teacher in Seoul for five years and is now working at the Palmer Museum of Art as a graduate assistant. She holds a M.Ed. in Museum Education and B.Ed. in Elementary Education from Seoul National University of Education in South Korea. She co-authored the book, *Museums in the Classroom: Theory and Practice of Museum Education Program,* in Korea. She is interested in critical disability studies, Asian American critical race theory, and feminist pedagogy in art education. Her ongoing dissertation work includes the stigmatization of women with scars and skin-clusive feminist art pedagogy.

Maya Ilayne Kirkland is a Junior at Texas Tech currently majoring in Psychology and triple minoring in English, General Business and Health Professions. After participating in a practicum in Women's and Gender Studies with Dra. Leslie C. Sotomayor II this past semester, she has decided to further her education and pursue her PhD. She enjoys philanthropic work and giving back to her community and hopes to utilize her degrees to make a true impact in the lives of others.

Soon Goo Lee is an Assistant Professor in the Department of Chemistry and Biochemistry at the University of North Carolina Wilmington (NC, USA). He received his Ph.D. from Washington University in St. Louis (MO, USA). His science research focuses on understanding the molecular basis of how macromolecules function in various metabolic pathways. His 'Genomic Identification–3D Structural Analysis–Protein Engineering' research strategy has made significant contributions to science, including over 35 published peer-reviewed papers and book chapters. As an educator, he firmly believes that "science" is a universal language readily available to interdisciplinary education teams. Collaborating with art educators, he has designed the STEAM (Science, Technology, Engineering, the Arts and Mathematics) program and integrated it into his courses and science outreach programs for local K–12 students. His educational endeavors have been published in 3 book chapters and peer-reviewed paper on the collaboration between 'biochemistry' and 'art-integration' courses.

Kyungeun Lim is an Assistant Professor at the School of Art and Design of Kennesaw State University. She worked as an Assistant Professor of Art Education at Northern Arizona University. She obtained her Ph.D. from Indiana University, double majoring in 1) Art Education in Curriculum & Instruction and 2) Comparative Education in Education Policy Studies. She received an M.A in Art Education and a B.F.A in Fine Art focusing on painting and Art Education from Seoul National University. She has been teaching arts and education from elementary school students to adults at schools, museums, and higher education institutions in traditional classroom settings and online classrooms—both synchronous and asynchronous. Lim's research interests are online art education, arts integration, STEAM, and digital technologies in K-16 art education.

Novea A. McIntosh, Ed.D. is an Assistant Professor, Coordinator of the Adolescent to Young Adult program and co-director of the Urban Teacher Academy in the School of Education and Health Sciences at the University of Dayton. Her scholarship focuses on culturally responsive pedagogy, intercultural competence, equity, assessment, and decolonization of education. Dr. McIntosh's scholarly work has been published in national and international journals. She also coaches and presents in her areas of research at conferences and provides professional development to in-service and pre-service teachers both nationally and internationally.

Rochonda L. Nenonene, Ph.D. is the First Year Experience Coordinator and Founding Co-Program Director of the Urban Teacher Academy at the University of Dayton. An Assistant Professor in the Department of Teacher Education, she teaches the introduction to the profession courses for undergraduate and graduate education candidates. Areas of research interests include: urban teacher preparation, culturally responsive teaching, equity, social-emotional learning and dispositions of teacher candidates. Dr. Nenonene conducts professional development for school districts on culturally responsive teaching, student engagement, classroom management, social-emotional learning and issues of equity.

Gina Gwen Palacios was born in Taft, Texas. She earned an MFA in Painting from the Rhode Island School of Design, a Post-Baccalaureate Certificate in Studio Art at Brandeis University, an MA from The University of Texas at Austin in Instructional Technology, a BA from Texas A&M University—Corpus Christi in TV/Film and an AA from Del Mar College in Radio/Television. Gina is an exhibiting artist, an Assistant Professor of Painting/Drawing and an Associate Director in the School of Art & Design at the University of Texas Rio Grande Valley in Brownsville, Texas.

Linda Hoeptner-Poling, PhD, Associate Professor, Art Education, Kent State University, is past president of NAEA's Women's Caucus, Distinguished Fellow for the Ohio Art Education Association, Brain Health Research Institute member at KSU, the 2018 OAEA Ohio Art Teacher of the Year, and the 2021 NAEA Women's Caucus Maryl Fletcher De Jong Awardee. She is a co-editor of the 2021 anthology, *National Art Education Association Women's Caucus Lobby Activism: Feminism(s) + Art* education and co-authored four editions of the *VSA Teacher Resource Guides: A Series of Visual Art Lesson Plans Designed to Engage Students with Disabilities,* published by the Kennedy Center.

Alexis Marie Ramos is Texas Born & Valley-raised and is originally from Weslaco, currently attends the University of Texas Rio Grande Valley, College of Fine Arts pursuing her MFA. Ramos received her BFA at UTRGV with a focus on ceramics. Under the mentorship of Professor Douglas Clark, she learned the art of lost-wax bronze casting and was engaged in the creation of several monumental sculptures in the Rio Grande Valley. Ramos also collaborated with artist Vilma Flores and The University of Texas Rio Grande Valley in bronze casting the new UTRGV ceremonial graduation mace and presidential medallion. Ramos received her Associates Degree at South Texas College and actively exhibits works in several of their galleries.

Glynnis Reed has been working as a professional visual artist and art educator for nearly two decades. Born in Los Angeles, she currently divides her time between her homes in Southern New Jersey and Pennsylvania where she attends The Pennsylvania State University as a doctoral candidate in the Art Education and Women's, Gender, and Sexuality Studies dual title degree program. Reed is the author of the book, *James Baldwin: Novelist and Critic,* from Enslow Publishing. You can view her art on her website: www.glynnisreed.com.

Rosalva Resendiz is an Associate Professor in the Department of Criminal Justice at The University of Texas Rio Grande Valley. Dr. Resendiz earned a Ph.D. in Sociology from Texas Woman's University. Dr. Resendiz identifies as Chicanx indigenous mestiza, focusing on social justice, critical criminology, critical race theory, decoloniality, postcolonial studies, Chicana feminism, and Mexican American/Border Studies. Dr. Resendiz is a native of the borderlands, her ancestry is Huichol/Wixarika, descendants of the semi-nomadic Guachichiles of the Gran Chichimeca.

Bianca Isabela Rodriguez is a second-generation native Houstonian. She is a first-year student at Texas Tech University majoring in Psychology and minoring in Women's and Gender Studies. Her dream is to become a therapist in the Houston area that focuses on helping women and people struggling with identity issues. She is passionate about working in a field that will benefit others throughout her community.

Yotam Ronen is a PhD candidate at the Department of Educational Studies, University of British Columbia. His research focuses on the global history of education, and the ways in which anarchist educators implement ideology in educational practice. Yotam's work is centered on reimagining education as a space of shared learning based on collective self-organization, free association, and mutual aid.

Adilene Rosales is a ceramic artist based in Mission, Texas. She received her BFA in studio art and minor in Psychology from The University of Texas Rio Grande Valley. She is currently working on her MFA at the same institution in studio 3D with a concentration in ceramics. Adilene's work focuses on raising awareness for Childhood cancer. Adilene's inspiration to raise awareness to a cause like such is based on her experience with cancer. Adilene uses clay because of the fragile states there is to this medium which represents how fragile our children are and yet the awareness given to this cause is not enough. Adilene's work focuses on statistics and the reality of this disease. Adilene hopes that her sculptures will make the viewer feel compelled and take action.

Nydia Salinas is a visual artist who grew up in between Progreso, Texas and Nvo. Progreso, Mexico. She received her Bachelor of Fine Arts degree from the University of Texas—Rio Grande Valley in 2020. Salinas recently participated in an International Artist Residency: Arquetopia (2021) on Pre-Columbian Ceramics in Puebla, Mexico thanks to the support of the Center for Latin American Arts at UTRGV. Salinas explores the dialect of the Rio Grande Valley and bases the conversation around her work on linguistic theories from text. Her ceramic vessels invite the viewer into a headspace where they can embrace their *tongue* and reject the idea of a "standard language." The dynamic of her upbringing—and the community she has encountered—is what inspired her journey in sharing the lived experiences of the people living on forced borderlands.

Leslie C. Sotomayor II is an artist, curator, and educator. Her dual Ph.Ds in Art Education and Women's, Gender, & Sexuality Studies from The Pennsylvania State University focuses on Gloria Anzaldúa's theories of conocimiento and autohistoria-teoría. Sotomayor situates Anzaldúa's theories as a feminist writing practice of theorizing one's experiences as transformative acts to guide her teaching methodology and curate curriculum for empowerment. She has curated numerous art exhibitions and publications including: *Testimonio in a Sculpture Series of Muñecas*: *Needlework: Forging Spaces for Making Through Conversation*: *Talking about Belonging and Survival* and her first book (2022), *Teaching In/Between: Curating Educational Spaces with Autohistoria-teoría and Conocimiento*. Her scholarship, curating and art embrace culturally responsive critical reflections for transformation.

Ricky Sullivan was born in Dos Palos, California, and raised in Mission, Texas in deep South Texas nestled against the border of Mexico. Growing up in a migrant family he often traveled back and forth from Texas to California for work. As a husband of 20 years and a proud father of 3, he has worked hard to complete his Bachelor of Fine Arts from The University of Texas Rio Grande Valley. He is a 3D artist with a concentration in ceramics. With a love for exploration and experimentation, the focus of his degree has been studio 3d sculpture and ceramics.

Samuel Jaye Tanner is an Assistant Professor of Literacy Education in The Pennsylvania State University System. His research concerns issues of whiteness, improvisation, and arts-based educational research. Sam's book *Whiteness, Pedagogy, and Youth in America* was recently selected as the recipient of the National Council of Teachers of English 2020 David H. Russell Award for Distinguished Research in the Teaching of English. Sam is also a creative writer. See more of Sam's work at: www.samjtanner.com

Maia Toteva is an assistant professor at Texas Tech University. She received her MA in medieval art history from Southern Methodist University and her PhD in modern and contemporary art history from the University of Texas at Austin. Her interests and teaching are interdisciplinary, encompassing the fields of art history, art education, and pedagogy. Dr. Toteva's research explores the intersections of contemporary art, language, and critical methodologies, with a particular emphasis on the entanglements of politics, identity, and ideology in the theory, practices, and forms of visual representation. She has published on topics spanning from global conceptualism to hybrid learning.

Paul Valadez grew up in Stockton, California and moved to San Francisco to pursue an art career. He earned his bachelor's degree in interdisciplinary art from the San Francisco Art Institute and his master's in studio art from University of North Carolina, Chapel Hill where he was awarded a Weiss Fellowship for Urban

Livability. Valadez is a professor in the Art department at the University of Texas, Rio Grande Valley, located at the U.S. Mexican border.

Mandy Wilson is a fine artist from Monroe, Louisiana. She attended Texas State University in San Marcos where she received a Bachelor of Fine Arts in Communication Design and an Art Teaching Certification. Currently, she resides in Texas with her husband and two children while pursuing a master's degree in 2D Art from the University of Texas Rio Grande Valley.

Made in the USA
Las Vegas, NV
01 February 2023

66651619R00111